Painting in the Grand Manner
The Art of Peter Frederick Rothermel
(1812-1895)

Painting in the Grand Manner
The Art of Peter Frederick Rothermel
(1812-1895)

Mark Thistlethwaite

September 9 through November 19, 1995

Brandywine River Museum

Chadds Ford, Pennsylvania

This publication and exhibition have been made possible by financial support from The Boeing Company, The Arcadia Foundation, The William Penn Foundation, and The Schwarz Gallery, Philadelphia.

Cover: (detail) and frontispiece:
(cat. 8) Patrick Henry in the House of Burgesses
of Virginia, Delivering His Celebrated
Speech against the Stamp Act, 1851
Courtesy of The Patrick Henry Memorial
Foundation, Brookneal, Virginia

A Brandywine River Museum Publication
© 1995 by the Brandywine Conservancy, Inc.
Library of Congress Catalogue Number: 95-75631

Edited by Catherine E. Hutchins
Designed by Géné E. Harris, Victoria Clark, and Glenn Weiser
Photographs for the Brandywine River Museum
by Rick Echelmeyer and Joseph Painter
Printed by Pearl Pressman Liberty Communications Group

Table of Contents

Preface

One hundred years after his death in 1895, Peter F. Rothermel's paintings have been long out of favor with most art historians and critics, a circumstance that testifies to shifting thought and taste. Greatly revered in his lifetime, Rothermel outlived the major age of history painting in America. That is not his fault and should not be his curse. His work is overdue for examination, analysis, and enjoyment. It is fine painting and the result of passion, knowledge, and highly developed skill.

The Brandywine River Museum is proud to present this exhibition and catalogue. It is appropriate that we do so; Rothermel has many links to the commitments of this museum, from the narrative qualities of his work to the regional dedication of this institution.

This exhibition was suggested by Mark Thistlethwaite, professor of art history at Texas Christian University, who served as guest curator for this museum's 1991 exhibition of paintings and drawings by William Tylee Ranney. Professor Thistlethwaite is a widely respected scholar whose research regarding Rothermel has been comprehensive and has produced the important results available on following pages. No museum ever worked with a finer or more enthusiastic guest curator, and we are deeply grateful to him.

His work was ably assisted in Chadds Ford by Gėnė E. Harris, curator of collections at the Brandywine River Museum, whose own enthusiasm for Rothermel moved the project forward in vital ways. Jean A. Gilmore, registrar, and Victoria A. Clark, assistant registrar, have also provided excellent assistance.

The Boeing Company is the much appreciated and generous corporate sponsor of the exhibition, as of previous events at this museum. Additional, essential support was provided by the William Penn Foundation, the Arcadia Foundation, and Schwarz Gallery, Philadelphia. Together they enabled us to present Rothermel's work in his region, the region in which these donors work as well.

No amount of curatorial effort or financial support could have produced this exhibition without the generosity of numerous lenders. They have gratitude from the Brandywine River Museum and should be honored by every visitor to the exhibition.

James H. Duff
Director

Acknowledgements

This exhibition could never have occurred without the enthusiastic support and expertise of James H. Duff and Ġėnė Harris, and the generosity of the many institutions and individuals who lent works of art and related materials. I appreciate the interest that Gil E. Pablo took in my work and the assistance he provided over many years. I am grateful for the editing skills of Catherine Hutchins and for the patience of Randi Thistlethwaite.

My work was also facilitated in a variety of ways by other helpful people, including William Ayres, James H. Elson, Robert Garwell, William H. Gerdts, Walter and Esther Gerhard, Holly K. Green, Mike Hammer, Florence Heydt, Joan Hendrix, Mattie Kelly, Kathleen Mendrey, Barbara Mitnick, Katherine Moody, Linda Ries, Joseph Rishel, Christine Schultz, Dale Schurr, Robert Schwarz, Paul D. Schweitzer, Robert Stewart, and Page Talbott.

Mark Thistlethwaite
Guest Curator

Lenders to the Exhibition

The Actors' Fund of America

Amon Carter Museum

Bowdoin College Art Museum

Thomas and Gail Bruhn

Descendant of P.F. Rothermel

Henry and Pearl Gerlach

Harry Ransom Humanities Research Center,
    The University of Texas at Austin

The Historical Society of Delaware

The Historical Society of Montgomery County

Kennedy Galleries, Inc., New York

The Library Company of Philadelphia

Lowe Art Museum, University of Miami

Moore College of Art and Design

Museum of American Art of the Pennsylvania
    Academy of the Fine Arts

Museum of Fine Arts, Boston

National Museum of American Art, Smithsonian Institution

Gil E. Pablo, M.D. Collection

The Patrick Henry Memorial Foundation

Pennsylvania State Archives, Harrisburg

Philadelphia Museum of Art

The Reading Public Museum

Rhode Island Historical Society

The Dale Schurr Family

Schwarz Gallery, Philadelphia

The State Museum of Pennsylvania

Robert Gordon Stewart

Union League of Philadelphia

Raymond and Diane Waltz

Woodmere Art Museum

Anonymous Lenders

Painting in the Grand Manner
The Art of Peter Frederick Rothermel
(1812-1895)

Fig. 1 *Peter F. Rothermel,* detail of undated photograph. Museum of American Art of the Pennsylvania Academy of the Fine Arts, Philadelphia

(cat. 2) *Columbus before the Queen,* 1841–1842, oil on canvas, 62⅜ × 50 in. National Museum of American Art, Smithsonian Institution

Preceding page: Detail of *Columbus before the Queen*

It has become a cliche for an exhibition to claim that an artist unknown today was, indeed, famous in his or her own time. Yet this is a truthful assertion in regard to Peter F. Rothermel (1812–1895, fig. 1). In 1884 historians J. Thomas Scharf and Thompson Westcott declared: "No Philadelphia artist is more widely known than Peter F. Rothermel."[1] Thomas Eakins, who knew Rothermel his whole life, considered him a "master"; art critic Earl Shinn claimed Rothermel was "the only poet in color belonging to the American school."[2] Given these and many other similar assessments, along with the impressive quality of so many of his paintings, why has this artist virtually disappeared from sight?

Two fundamental reasons account for Rothermel's eclipse. First, Rothermel was a Philadelphian; consequently, he did not receive the wide attention throughout his career that a comparable New York artist would have. Philadelphia critics constantly supported Rothermel's art, but New York art writers, who praised his early work, grew increasingly hostile and, especially from the 1860s on, belittled his efforts. Writing for the *New-York Daily Tribune* in 1866, Clarence Cook referred to Rothermel as "the pride of the Quaker City" and snidely assured his readers that Philadelphia's "admiration for that artist, which certainly is provincial, will be outgrown."[3] Years later Cook continued to denigrate the city and the artist, remarking that Rothermel enjoys considerable fame only "at home in Philadelphia, where if anywhere, honors are easy."[4] Philadelphia artists were keenly aware that New Yorkers looked down upon them. Xanthus Smith, thinking of showing work in New York in 1874, expressed his "doubts as to how it might be received. Anything from Philadelphia in New York, you know that would be a hamper at the outset."[5] Twenty-one years later, shortly after the nearly simultaneous deaths of Rothermel and Thomas Hovenden, a writer for a Philadelphia newspaper caustically observed:

The New York newspapers have had no comment to make upon the deaths of Thomas Hovenden and P. F. Rothermel or upon their place in the world of American art. These men were more widely known than any other two American artists. Their work and position were of the first importance. The obliviousness of the New York editors to their existence is doubtless due to the fact that the artists did not live in New York. Such extreme provincialism must be more or less disadvantageous even to the New York press.[6]

Rothermel's art never received the critical support in New York that would have enhanced his reputation nationally and perhaps secured it posthumously.

The other major reason why Rothermel's reputation disappeared centers on the type of art in which he specialized: grand manner history painting. Rothermel worked in a style popular in the early nineteenth century, but one that after midcentury, and especially after the Civil War, was increasingly passé. Longer than any other nineteenth-century American artist Rothermel continued the tradition of grand style history painting. When he died, he was described as "the Last Artist of the Older School," and a colorist "not in touch with the latter-day impressionists…[thus] his pictures are not just now in fashion with all those who are incapable of understanding anything that does not look like Claude Monet."[7] To modernists, Rothermel's grand academic and narrative art looked woefully outmoded and inconsequential.

These two biases—one against Philadelphia and the other against history painting—condemned Rothermel and his paintings to oblivion. Today, a time of reconsidering received notions, the moment is right to look anew at the art of Peter F. Rothermel.

The son of innkeepers and farmers, Rothermel was born in Nescopeck, Luzerne County, Pennsylvania, on July 8, 1812. His birth date has frequently been given as 1817, and even the artist confessed that, having a poor memory for dates, he was not absolutely sure of the year (although he knew 1817 to be too late); however, "1812" is inscribed on his gravestone in Woodlands Cemetery, Philadelphia, and is the date cited in a recent genealogy.[8]

The artist's early years are obscure, but one story has the "budding genius" manifesting talent in childhood by painting a sign for his father's hotel.[9] As a teenager he learned surveying from John Stauffer of Boyertown, for whom he may have embellished maps.[10] Around 1832 Rothermel moved to Philadelphia and worked as a sign painter. Three or four years after arriving in the city he saw his first exhibition of art, in an apartment over Mrs. Hobson's stationery store on Chestnut Street, following which he studied drawing with John Rubens Smith and painting with Bass Otis.[11] Initially the young artist specialized in portraiture, and his first recorded exhibited work, *Portrait of a Gentleman*, appeared in the 1838 Artists' Fund Society exhibition. Although Rothermel continued to paint portraits throughout his career, in the 1840s he turned to history painting, the mode upon which he built his reputation.

In the nineteenth century, "history painting" was a fairly broad term used to denote narrative compositions that were didactic in character and depicted significant figures and action. Subject matter might be drawn from history, mythology, literature, or the Bible. As it evolved from the Renaissance through the eighteenth century, history painting attained the status of being the highest mode of painting, with "grand manner" designating a dramatic combination of elevated content and romantically idealized style. By the 1840s history painting still occupied a premier position, but increasingly in principle only. More commonplace subjects rendered in a more realistic style were displacing it.

Rothermel was one of the few American artists committed to perpetuating traditional history painting; another was Emanuel Leutze, the creator of that most famous of all American history paintings, *Washington Crossing the Delaware* (1851). A number of similarities link the two artists. Leutze was German born, while Rothermel was of German descent. Both began their art studies in Philadelphia, and they may have been in John Rubens Smith's drawing class at the same time. The two lived in the same Philadelphia neighborhood. Both went to Dusseldorf to study. Both rendered a variety of historical subjects. And both painted dynamic theatrical compositions. Despite these similarities, differences do distinguish their art. Rothermel's range of historical subjects is greater. Leutze's prolonged study in Dusseldorf defined his style; Rothermel's style was set by the time he briefly visited Dusseldorf. Leutze's art was noted for its well-defined and detailed forms; Rothermel's for its coloristic effects. Leutze represented the German school; Rothermel combined the influences of British and French artists. For contemporaries, Leutze represented a natural-born talent who "leaped to eminence"; Rothermel "climbed" taking "slow, but steady and unfaltering steps, and this gradual ascent was the keystone of his career, marking a resolution and an indomitable patience that never flagged."[12] That rise began in the early 1840s, as Rothermel seriously turned to grand history painting.

The artist's first large history painting was the 1842 *Columbus before the Queen* (cat. 2), but the painting he considered his "first great success" was the 1843 *De Soto Discovering the Mississippi River* (fig. 2), which he exhibited at the Pennsylvania Academy of the Fine Arts in Philadelphia and then the National Academy of Design in New York, where the American Art-Union purchased it.[13] Both early works display the idealized compositions and the colorful and expressive rendering that were to mark the artist's oeuvre. They, like his images of Cortés, also from the 1840s, perpetuate a romantically elevated vision of exploration, appropriate in this age of "Manifest Destiny." Rothermel, one writer noted, "seems to have conceived the grandeur of high civilization as contrasted with barbarism and the passions that the finding of a new world was calculated to inspire in the minds of the discoverers."[14] Throughout his art, Rothermel's images perpetuate the drama and grandeur of history.

During the 1840s Rothermel exhibited six paintings a year on average. The wide range of the subject matter in these works is both impressive and typical. For example, in 1845 he exhibited four portraits, a Biblical scene (*Prayer*

Fig. 2 Peter F. Rothermel, *DeSoto Discovering the Mississippi,* ca. 1843, oil on canvas, 50⅛ × 63⅛ in. St. Bonaventure University Art Collection, part of the Doctor T.E. Hanley Collection

of Tobit), a literary subject (*The Palmer's Return*) and three historical episodes (*Mrs. Shubrick Protecting an American Soldier, Surrender of Guatemozin* [cat. 5] and *Washington Prescribing for the Poor Widow*).[15] It was probably about this time that John Neagle publicly responded to "hypercritical" claims:

> Look you, gentlemen, none of us are perfect. Perhaps Rothermel has faults, but his good qualities are so strong that I perceive them only. He is a master in composition, his color is glorious, he always tells his story well, and he is altogether the best historical painter we have. What more do you want?[16]

The 1840s also saw Rothermel become a significant figure in the Philadelphia art community. He opened a studio in "Art Row," on Sansom Street below Eighth Street. Members of the Artists' Fund Society elected him their vice-president in 1844.[17] From 1847 (the same year the National Academy of Design elected him an honorary member) to 1855 Rothermel served as a director of the Pennsylvania Academy of the Fine Arts, where for a time, he oversaw the academy's school.[18] He played a dominant role in structuring the academy's curriculum along the lines of the Ecole des Beaux-Arts in Paris.[19] When he helped initiate a life class at the academy he also suggested a code of regulations, which included no conversing between model and student, no smoking, and maintaining the strictest order.[20] The high opinion held of Rothermel by the academy's board of directors is indicated by his appointment to three of its four standing committees: Academy, Exhibition, and Instruction. Illustrations by him, engravings after his paintings, and notices about him published in a variety of gift books and journals, including *Godey's Lady's Book, Eclectic Magazine*, and *Sartain's Union Magazine of Literature and Art*, established his artistic reputation in popular circles. *Sartain's* pronounced: "Rothermel belongs to the very foremost rank of living historical painters in this country, and in the opinion of many of those best able to form a correct judgment, takes the lead of all."[21]

During the 1850s Rothermel's fame continued to spread as he created some of his best and most widely known work. One composition attracting considerable attention was *Murray's Defence of Toleration* (fig. 3). Based on Walter Scott's *History of Scotland*, the painting was "one of the chief ornaments" of the 1850 annual exhibition at the National Academy of Design and was purchased the following year by the American Art-Union.[22] This "correctly drawn, harmoniously colored, and nicely balanced…picture will confer great distinction on the artist," predicted one critic. [23] Another opined that Rothermel could become "*the* historical painter of America."[24] Yet, the theme of religious toleration—the prior of Saint Andrews (later, the earl of Murray) protecting Mary Queen of Scots at her devotions from zealous Protestants—divided Rothermel's audience. Philadelphia was in a period of religious turmoil which included anti-Catholic rioting in 1844. One city newspaperman suggested that Rothermel's painting evoked "an incident which we all know and should lose nothing in forgetting"; however, another journalist cited the current Catholic-Protestant antagonism as the very reason not to dismiss the painting.[25] The divided reaction may account for the low price the painting brought at the American Art-Union sale of 1852.[26]

In 1851 a most intriguing work by Rothermel appeared, *The Laborer's Vision of Human Progress*. Unlocated today and with no known reproductions of it, this allegorical painting must be visualized from written accounts. It was described as a big composition "in a style entirely different, with a character unlike Rothermel's other works." The commentator continued:

Fig. 3 Alfred Jones after Peter Rothermel, *Murray's Defense of Toleration*, etching, *American Art-Union Bulletin,* September 1851. Library Company of Philadelphia

> Upon the barren highway, a worn-out and exhausted woman, child in arms, sinks down to die. The husband and father, spade in hand, raises his eyes upward from the affliction and despair of one dearer to him than himself; and sees before him a landscape, glowing with the glory of sunset. Of what value to these starved wretches are the beauties of Nature now? He casts his eyes to heaven, and the keen eye of Hope, piercing the clouds of the present, sees a glorious vision, causing a new fire to gleam up amid the dying embers of his trust. There he beholds a glorious picture, upborne by coming Time. The dear ones now perishing are beatified; Tyranny is vanquished; and he himself is about to received, from the Supreme Lord of the Labourer, the reward of his toil. Hope revives; the dignity of manhood once more enters and erects his form; and the soul wraps itself in the glorious promise. The picture is ether; ethereal; and, in conception and execution, is one of the most sublime.[27]

The work reflected the popularity of John Bunyan's *Pilgrim's Progress*, and it implicitly addressed the increasingly vexing question of slavery.

Bunyan's seventeenth century "metaphysical narrative" profoundly affected Americans (as the Reverend Mr. Belcher asked the readers of *Sartain's*: "who has not read and admired his 'Pilgrim's Progress'?") and Rothermel explicitly based at least one painting on *Pilgrim's Progress* (cat. 47). A kindred spirit animates Bunyan's pilgrim and Rothermel's laborer: both look to the reward of "a home in the celestial city." Along with this Bunyanesque sensibility, descriptions of the painting as depicting both "Tyranny vanquished," and "the coming of a better day to the children of toil" suggest the antislavery sentiments.[28] Intense debates over the Fugitive Slave Act of 1850 took place in Philadelphia, long a center of the Underground Railroad.[29] Although we do not know Rothermel's intentions in *The Laborer's Vision of Human Progress*, its potential political dimensions are fascinating and provocative.

The lengthy description of the painting came at the conclusion of a

Fig. 4 Thomas Dunn English, M.D., "Peter F. Rothermel," *Sartain's Union Magazine of Literature and Art*, January 1852, 13.

Thomas Dunn English's 1852 biography of the artist, an article that signaled and contributed to the artist's rise to prominence. English began his account by describing the artist (fig. 4): "a tall, gaunt, and spare man, with blue, incredulous eyes, and bronzed, irrevocable features" who one might think would be "a lawyer, or a physician, or an engineer, or the projector of a western town" because he shows no signs of the "dreaminess" associated with the "*caste*." After supplying detailed information about the artist and his work (which often has been repeated in biographical essays), English offered a stirring conclusion: "That he may live many years, to shed lustre upon art and increase his own fame, is the wish of all who admire genius, and desire its own recompense in its own way."[30]

This essay appeared, probably not coincidentally, just prior to the well-publicized exhibition of the artist's *Patrick Henry in the House of Burgesses in Virginia, Delivering His Celebrated Speech against the Stamp Act* (cat. 8). The Art Union of Philadelphia commissioned this work, truly one of Rothermel's masterpieces. The large painting, with its high drama, powerful narrative, and colorful painterliness, wonderfully exemplifies the artist's grand manner. Art Union members received a copy of Alfred Jones's engraving of the painting (cat. 8b), a print that the Philadelphia *Inquirer* later claimed hangs "in so many American households that it is doubtful if any other American artist was so widely known."[31] When the painting was exhibited in the Rotunda of the United States Capitol in 1852, twenty Philadelphia artists, including Thomas Sully, Rembrandt Peale, John Neagle, J. R. Lambdin, John Sartain, William Trost Richards, Samuel Waugh and Christian Schuessele, petitioned Congress to commission Rothermel to produce a national work.[32]

Their petition, dated May 11, 1852, deemed Rothermel "an Artist really deserving of the high rank he holds as an historical painter."[33] Senator James Cooper of Pennsylvania introduced the petition to Congress, proclaiming Rothermel "one of the most eminent historical painters of the country."[34] On June 8 the Senate considered Cooper's resolution calling for commissions be given to Rothermel as well as to G. P. A. Healy and Emanuel Leutze.[35] Nothing came of the resolution. Why remains unknown; however, a contributing factor may be that Montgomery Meigs, who came to control Capitol art commissions in 1853, disliked Rothermel's art. Indeed he dismissed *Patrick Henry*, by rather amazingly terming it a "sketch, as though [Rothermel] had not the industry or skill to paint a finished picture."[36]

In Philadelphia, meanwhile, Rothermel's patronage grew. The particular view of history and culture in his colorfully romantic images found a sympathetic audience among the city's most eminent and well-to-do businessmen, bankers, civic leaders, manufacturers, and art collectors. During an era of political and social unrest and change, Rothermel's grand manner history paintings appealed to their notions of high art and tradition. In the 1860s many of his patrons were, like him, to join the newly formed Union League, which quickly became the leading club in Philadelphia and "a bastion of Republican respectability."[37] The organization grew out of antislavery sentiments, and "its inspiration was pure and disinterested patriotism; its foundation-stone was devotion to the Union; its founders and fortifiers were the true sons of the founders and upbuilders of the nation."[38]

Among the surviving correspondence and records involving the artist and his well-to-do Philadelphia patrons is a fascinating multivolume diary kept by Joseph Sill, a merchant, amateur painter, and art collector.[39] Early on Sill admired Rothermel's raw talent and in 1841 wrote, he "is improving rapidly in his art, and promises to be a finished artist—his coloring at present is a little too warm, and his drawing a little extravagant, but he has evidently got the genuine taste and feeling for his art and will improve rapidly."[40] Sill and Rothermel saw each other often, and in 1851, at which time Rothermel was working on *Antonio's Letter* for Sill (the entries are detailed at cat. 53), they spent three days in New York looking at art. They went especially to examine Carl Friedrich Lessing's *Martyrdom of Huss* at the Dusseldorf Gallery, but both found that it did not live up to their expectations.[41] The following year Sill urged Rothermel to go abroad for two or three years, a suggestion the artist planned to carry out the following spring.[42] It was not, however, until August 1856, that Rothermel and his family sailed to Europe. Sill, who undoubtedly would have enjoyed learning the artist's impressions of Europe and assessing his progress, had by then died.

To help pay for the 1856 sojourn Rothermel secured a number of commissions. A surviving notebook, which dates from the years 1856 to 1859, lists patrons and prices, including:

> E. W. Clark. subject[s?] of agreeable nature—Choice Mine $250
> Wm. B. Johnston subject light my choice 250
> Jos. Patterson. Serious. suggested historical or otherwise 4 a.[@]
>   5[00]
> Abt. Cummings Topsy & Eva—or my own choice 250
> John Rice Paul before Felix 500
> C. Macalester Something in the life of Napoleon or of that character 250
> Col C. G. Childs Widow at my Grave 150.[43]

Rothermel recorded other commissions and sales throughout the book. By the end of 1858 he had sold several works to foreign nobility: Grand Duchess Helena of Russia purchased an original sketch of Lear for $200 and *Fountain at Genazzano*, also for $200; Count Conchilef bought *Saint Agnes* for $1500 and *The Virtuoso* for $250; and Prince Kozebue commissioned *Rubens and Van Dyck* at $400.[44] A correspondent to the *Crayon* noted that Rothermel was "greatly admired and patronised by the Russian nobility" and later joked:

A large detachment of artistic militia went off with Rothermel last June, and have not been heard of since. Some fears are entertained that they may have enlisted in Russia, under the Duchess Helena, of whom they received commissions last year; but we hope this is not the case.[45]

James Vansyckle contracted to pay Rothermel $1200 per year for three years in exchange for not more than four nor less than two paintings each of the three years. The size of the pictures was "to *suit* the *subject* and not to be *repeated*," and Vansyckle was to be given all the preparatory sketches. In May 1858 the artist received the first year's installment.[46]

Rothermel traveled extensively throughout Europe—London, Paris, Dusseldorf, Munich, Genoa, Florence, Venice—but stayed in Rome and nearby Genazzano for two years.[47] When he arrived in Rome in 1857, he joined an impressive contingent of American writers, including William Cullen Bryant, Nathaniel Hawthorne, Herman Melville, William Wetmore Story and dozens of American artists including William H. Beard, Albert Bierstadt, Sanford Gifford, and Worthington Whittredge, with whom he hiked the Alban Hills.[48] As for the Italians, Rothermel found them "to be a very liberal set, and I was handsomely treated by them."[49] In Genazzano his studio was in the old Colonna castle and consisted of a suite of apartments that had been used by Pope Martin V when Genazzano had been the court town.[50]

Before sailing home he visited Paris again, where three of his works were hung in the Salon and gained him an honorable mention.[51] The Paris correspondent for the *New-York Daily Tribune* reported: "MR. ROTHERMEL'S works have been duly noticed by the Paris as well as some of the London critics, and all agree in praising the artist's unusual strength and harmony of color."[52] While in Paris, Rothermel recorded in his notebook his impressions of what he saw in the Louvre. Most of these are brief, but Thomas Couture's *Romans of the Decadence* (1847) elicited a paragraph:

A Classic composition of great force. too precise in arrangement. *Well drawn* and portions of the Colour good, but as a general thing[?] lacks purity and is devoid of Earnestness and vivacity of Expressions. impresses one as more the result of Tallent than Genius and is yet a work of great value. Compared with nature his flesh is pale cadaverous brittle or statuesque. It is little *if any* more fleshy than his marble.

Eugene Delacroix's *Dante and Virgil* he termed "Grand in sentiment. parts exceedingly good in colour drawing. *Infernal.*"[53]

Delacroix was an artist Rothermel admired and one with whom writers linked him.

Born with the subtle sense of tone-harmony of an Eugene Delacroix, [Rothermel] is not much more accurate than Delacroix in the pedantry of anatomic detail, the rectitude of architectural and constructive lines....We have heard Rothermel criticised, and even with acerbity; artists of the Delacroix order especially invite the animadversions of wiseheads.; but we confess, on those occasions, the party we pitied was the critic, not Rothermel.[54]

Rothermel's assessment of the French master was pithier: "Of all the Colour I have yet seen Delacroix is the best of the Moderns."[55]

Returning to Philadelphia in July 1859, Rothermel renewed his participation in various art organizations, including the Pennsylvania Academy of the Fine Arts, which elected him a Pennsylvania Academician in 1860. (Later, he served as president of the academy's council of academicians.) In 1864 he was elected president of the Artists' Fund Society. During this time he taught, but almost nothing is known of this aspect of his career except through comments written by one of his pupils, Eliza Haldeman.

This young woman became a friend of Mary Cassatt when they both enrolled at the Pennsylvania Academy of the Fine Arts in the 1860. The classes usually met without an instructor, so most students engaged well-known artists for private lessons.[56] It is not clear when Eliza Haldeman began studying with Rothermel in his studio, but by February 16, 1863, she was writing her father that she is at Rothermel's "fully started and like it very much. I know I am learning a great deal."[57] She was copying at an old man's head (a study by Rothermel made in Rome) and described the class of eight as pleasant but with "very little talking."[58] Rothermel impressed her: "he puts me in mind of Rubens who he is said to imitate and I think he would use street scrapping if it would give him an efect....I think he is the best teacher I could have had, he certainly is a great artist."[59] (Haldeman was correct, Rothermel did indeed admire Rubens. In a letter from London, Rothermel noted that "Rubens in the National Gallery is wonderfull for the purity and force of his colour and fullness and admirable arrangement of his forms, in fact so far as I can see he is by far my favorite in point of colour.")[60] By February 26 Haldeman was conversant with Rothermel's technique:

[H]e has a different mode of laying on the tints for each kind of material....He relieves his compositions entirely by effect and contrast of color not by shadows and he is peculiarly noted for the atmosphere he puts into the foreground of his pictures so that two figures standing quite near each other are as distinct as in life, as if you could put your hand between them or walk round them with ease, and though some figures are entirely in shadow those that *are* in light have no dense shadows. I believe it is generally supposed that a shadow ought not have white in it. Now I don't think he ever makes one in which it does not enter, at least all *flesh* shadows are so...where ever he can possibly put white, there you will see it. Asphatum is another of his chief colors, and many of his tints which make conoisseurs wonder are composed of the mixture of these two, any other color entering to tint it.[61]

Haldeman's focus on Rothermel's color, his best known stylistic trait, is logical. What is unexpected is the attention she gave to describing his drawing technique:

> There is wonderful *drawing* in all his pictures and people who say he can't draw don't know anything. He knows anatomy well, never attends disections [but works from a muscle-labeled anatomic cast]….He always draws his figures nude and clothes them as he paints, it is the greatest pleasure immaginable to stand behind him and see them *being dressed*, an old roman will put on his toga and sandles, a ladie her boddice and skirt, a beggar his torn rags, and a king his crown with the same ease that you would slide into your wrapper in *our* old studio at home.[62]

Drawing formed an integral aspect of Rothermel's academic approach; however, a letter Haldeman wrote from France five years later suggests that Rothermel did not actually paint *from* the figure: "We were at Barbizon last week but [Cassatt] was not pleased with the Master she intended taking. You can imagine the horror we were seized with on hearing he painted without models, a sort of french Rothermel."[63] Similarly, Thomas Eakins, who owned some life study drawings by Rothermel (cats. 38–43), noted: "Rothermel did not follow his models closely and took different phases of character from them."[64] Haldeman's and Eakins's comments remind us of the obvious: Rothermel's art is one of idealization not realism. His penchant for not painting from models may account for the repetition of figures that occur in many of Rothermel's compositions.

One of the highlights of Rothermel's career was his participation in Philadelphia's Great Central Fair. This major event, held in Logan Square between June 7 and June 28, 1864, was one of thirty fund-raising fairs held during the Civil War in support of the United States Sanitary Commission, an organization providing medical supplies and clothing to Union field hospitals.[65] The fair raised over a million dollars in relief funds by presenting a vast array of displays and artifacts. The "most remarkable single feature" of the fair, according to its own newspaper, *Our Daily Fare*, was the collection of paintings, "the largest ever exhibited in America."[66] Of the 1,400 paintings exhibited in the 500–foot-long gallery, 20 were by Peter F. Rothermel. The number alone, more than any other artist, testifies to Rothermel's artistic eminence and his political affiliations. Less than two months earlier, on April 9, he had been elected by a group of his peers as chairman of a subcommittee of Philadelphia artists, which functioned under the art committee chaired by his friend and patron Joseph Harrison, Jr. He, like the artist, was a member of the Union League of Philadelphia, an organization that helped promote the Great Central Fair. Of the fourteen lenders (including the artist) of Rothermel paintings, ten were, or would soon be, members of the all-male Union League, and two were women. The coincidence of his highly regarded art being in the hands of collectors supportive of Great Central Fair made the event a showcase for his art.

Two years after the fair, Rothermel received the commission for his largest and most ambitious painting, *The Battle of Gettysburg: Pickett's Charge* (cat. 27).[67] Commissioned by the Commonwealth of Pennsylvania for $25,000, the huge canvas—sixteen by nearly thirty-two feet—occupied the artist from 1867 to 1870. Much of this time was given over to research and gathering information from participants in the battle; nonetheless, according to Thomas Eakins, who frequently dropped by to watch the artist at work, the actual painting process took longer than eighteen months.[68] When it was finished another difficulty became publicly apparent: legislators had failed to provide a proper building in Harrisburg to house the painting. As Rothermel put it, "[the state] has an elephant on its hands and no available stablery for it."[69] After elaborate unveiling ceremonies at the Academy of Music in Philadelphia, the work traveled to Boston, Chicago (where it suffered damage during the Great Fire of 1871), and Pittsburgh (where repairs were made). In 1873, it and four companion compositions that were part of the commission, became the focal point of a temporary gallery in Fairmount Park, Philadelphia, which was again instigated and supported by Joseph Harrison, Jr. The work moved in 1876 to Memorial Hall, where it appeared conspicuously in the International Centennial Exposition.

There the New York critics "savagely abused and malignantly reviled" the painting for what they considered its inappropriate subject ("an unsuitable reminder…of discords of the past") and poor technique ("about the size and shape of a drop curtain and of the same order of merit").[70] The reporter for *Appleton's Journal* bluntly asserted: "The picture is bad in every sense."[71] Clarence Cook, who wrote for the *New-York Tribune* and intensely disliked Rothermel's art, ranked *The Battle of Gettysburg: Pickett's Charge* as the worst painting in the Centennial.[72] Joaquin Miller of the *Independent* deemed it a bloody monstrosity and claimed its appeal was to "the crowd of verdant country folk" and that "popularity, in a crowd so vast and uncultured as this same, means vulgarity."[73] (Miller's description notwithstanding, the painting shows remarkably little blood, considering the ferocity of the scene.) The painting did have its defenders: "There is nothing in the art gallery of the Centennial Exhibition which can have a better claim to a place than Mr. Rothermel's battle-piece"; "The picture is a powerful treatment of a very difficult subject, and the best art judges long ago decided in its favor."[74] Author William Dean

Howells admitted, "I had a horrific interest in the spectacle, almost as large as the canvas, which covers the whole end of one room; and I thought the rebels were fighting hard, and, if they were dying, were dying bravely."[75]

The monumental canvas remained on view in Memorial Hall for many years. In 1887 it (along with eight other Rothermel paintings) traveled to London as part of an American art exhibition.[76] John Sartain, commissioner for this exhibition, subsequently recalled that the Commonwealth of Pennsylvania agreed to send the huge painting "as the artist was still living, the work, if lost, would be reproduced by him from studies and photographs of its parts and as a whole, it was insured for thirty thousand dollars."[77] Finally, in 1894 the painting was finally installed in Harrisburg.

The intense negative response to *The Battle of Gettysburg: Pickett's Charge* reflects the generally unfavorable critical response to Rothermel's works from the 1860s on. Writers increasingly regarded his art as old fashioned and referred to his paintings as exaggeratedly dramatic "old soldiers." One author dubbed *Christ and the Doctors* (cat. 16), "the Deck of the Great Eastern in a Storm."[78] Objecting to Rothermel's penchant for the melodramatic, a *New York Evening Post* critic facetiously described Rothermel's *Roland and Agatha* (also known as *House by the Sea*) thusly:

> a blood-red horizon, a man in a boat grasping a namby-pamby young woman's hand, a second young woman near the bow, an aged, bearded grandfather in the stern, a horned Mephistopheles at the helm, impossible water, towering cliffs, luridness, Bowery Theatre, act fifth, last scene, he is going to leap, hold your breath![79]

Another lambasted *Hypatia* as "utterly inexcusable in its badness," and suggested "the absurd pretensions of Mr. Rothermel's admirers... [were] confined, we should suppose, to Philadelphia."[80] The vehemence of such remarks not only reflects the New York reception of Rothermel's mature art of the grand manner, but also relates to a general shift in aesthetic taste, which increasingly found little to admire in traditional history painting.[81]

Favorable commentary did occur, to be sure, and almost always it emphasized Rothermel's skill as a colorist. It also tended to be as hyperbolic as negative criticism:

> Mr. Rothermel is *the* American colorist, and in his coloring, as in the other characteristics of his style, he is original and distinctively American. None of the European color masters can approach him in the peculiar qualities that give his pictures their greatest value.[82]

Owing to poor health, Rothermel virtually ceased painting in the mid 1880s, and he spent his last years at his country home, Grassmere, Linfield, Pennsylvania (fig. 5). The Art Club of Philadelphia honored him in 1890 with "a brilliant affair" that attracted about 400 people, and featured "thirteen of the paintings, which years ago made Mr. Rothermel known to lovers of art, far and wide."[83] An old friend—painter Russell Smith—who could not attend sent his regrets. He recalled a time

> at the Academy where I wandered wondering at the acres of canvas, grand [?] gold frames, the crimson masses of drapery and the careful and expensive means used to impress us with the vast achievement made in the new Realistic style in art. I *was* somewhat dazed, and leaving the southwest gallery…your Christian Martyrs [see cat. 18a] flashed upon me with a force and sence of delight that woke me up again to the wonderfull superiority of real true Art—such massive grouping—such colour and splendid light and shade; and if I had been staggered for a moment, I was again, and forever, reassured.
>
> I hope you are very well and philosopher enough to rest content with the good you have already done; and if the world here about us is blind to the interests of good art it is no fault of yours.[84]

Rothermel, like Smith, must have felt distanced from the art of the day, in which "the most riotous kind of license [that is to say, impressionism] is taken by artists in a mad endeavor to be 'up to date.' "[85]

Peter F. Rothermel died on August 15, 1895.[86] Virtually every obituary (and dozens appeared) acknowledged that "with him passes away the veteran of that sturdy style of historical painting now neglected and out of vogue."[87] Although "guided by certain principles and ideals and…painted in the spirit of the laws laid down by the masters before him," Rothermel's art was then out of step with modernist taste.[88] Yet, as one writer claimed, "measured by the value of his numerous works of merit and importance his career has been one of the most successful known to the history of art in this country."[89]

As we look at this significant body of Rothermel's paintings, drawings, and engravings after his work—brought together for the first time in a hundred years—it is difficult not to be fascinated by the ambitiousness of Rothermel's vision and impressed by the character, power, and beauty of his art.

Fig. 5   Postcard of Peter F. Rothermel's Home and Studio, Linfield, Montgomery County. Collection of the Historical Society of Montgomery County.

The Artist Rothermel's Home and Studio, E. D. Miller Publisher, Parkerford, Pa.

Notes

1 J. Thomas Scharf and Thompson Westcott, *History of Philadelphia…*(Philadelphia: L. H. Everts, 1884), 3: 2327n.

2 "Hovenden and Rothermel," *Press* (Philadelphia), August 17, 1895, p. 4. E. S. [Earl Shinn], "Private Art-Collections of Philadelphia: I.—Mr. James L. Claghorn's Gallery," *Lippincott's Magazine of Literature, Science, and Education* 9 (April 1872): 441. Eakins was connected to Rothermel by the marriage of Rothermel's daughter, Blanche, to James Macdowell, who was the older brother of Eakins's wife Susan. For many years, the Rothermels and Macdowells were neighbors on Race Street in Philadelphia.

3 C[larence] C[ook], "An Art Journey," *New-York Daily Tribune*, August 21, 1866, p. 2.

4 Clarence Cook, "Fine Arts—National Academy of Design," *New-York Tribune*, April 4, 1880, p. 7.

5 Xanthus Smith to Commo. B. S. Osbon, December 17, 1874, Smith Family Papers, Archives of American Art, Smithsonian Institution. For a brief discussion of the Philadelphia-New York rivalry, see Jean Taylor Baxter, "Burdens and Rewards: Some Issues for American Artists, 1865–1875," Ph.D. diss., University of Maryland, 1988, pp. 96, 245.

6 Clipping from the Philadelphia *Inquirer*, August 19, 1895, Scrapbooks of Thomas Hovenden, Archives of American Art, Smithsonian Institution.

7 "P. F. Rothermel Dead," *Public Ledger* (Philadelphia), August 16, 1895, p. 1; "Another Artist Passes Away," *Press*, August 16, 1895, p. 1.

8 "A Venerable Artist," *Public Ledger*, March 19, 1890, p. 3. "The artist has a disgracefully bad memory of dates and figures" (Thomas Dunn English, "Peter F. Rothermel," *Sartain's Union Magazine of Literature and Art* 10 [January 1852]: 14); Joseph A. Meiser, Jr., ed., *Rothermel Families in America* (Newtown Square, Pa.: Harrowood Books, 1989), p. 627.

9 Henry Wilson Ruoff, ed., *Biographical and Portrait Cyclopedia of Montgomery County, Pennsylvania…* (Philadelphia: Biographical Publishing Co., 1895), p. 578.

10 John Stauffer was a surveyor, politician, and associate justice of the Berks County Court. A genealogical study claims that Rothermel worked in Stauffer's Boyertown, Pennsylvania, office illustrating deeds with drawings of houses, credits Stauffer as the "first to discover the genius that possessed the mind of the celebrated painter," and maintains that Rothermel's first portrait was of Judge Stauffer (A. J. Fretz, *A Genealogical Record of the Descendants of Henry Stauffer and Other Stauffer Pioneers…*[Harleysville, Pa.: Harleysville News, 1899], pp. 211–12; portraits of Justice and Mrs. Stauffer face p. 259). Although this information occurs nowhere else, its validity is probable; Abner K. Stauffer, son of John Stauffer, attended Rothermel's funeral ("Artist Rothermel Died," *Reading Weekly Eagle*, August 24, 1895, p. 1). I thank Holly K. Green for bringing the book and obituary to my attention.

11 "A Venerable Artist," *Public Ledger*, p. 3. That article cites an 1890 interview in which Rothermel spoke of studying only with Smith; however, in an 1871 letter to George Lowell Austen (Joseph Downs Collection of Manuscripts and Printed Ephemera, Library, Winterthur), Rothermel indicated that he also took painting from Otis. One of Rothermel's students reported that Rothermel had "studied about three months with Otis, he says it took him six to get rid of the faults he gave him." (Eliza Haldeman to Samuel Haldeman, February 26, 1863, Archives, Pennsylvania Academy of the Fine Arts).

12 "Sartain Talks of the Dead Artists," *Press*, August 18, 1895, p. 7. Sartain had first voiced these sentiments 46 years earlier; see "Notices of Arts and Artists," *Sartain's Union Magazine of Literature and Art* 4 (June 1849): 414.

13 "A Venerable Artist," *Public Ledger*, p. 3.

14 M[oses] Auge, *Lives of the Eminent Dead and Biographical Notices of Prominent Living Citizens of Montgomery County, Pa.* (Norristown: M. Auge, 1879), p. 427.

15 All were shown at the Artists' Fund Society, except *Surrender of Guatemozin*, which was exhibited at the National Academy of Design. In 1845 Rothermel also painted *Abraham Casting Out Hagar and Ishmael* (see cat. 6) and *Ruth and Boaz* (see cat. 35).

16 As cited in Thomas Fitzgerald, "John Neagle: The Artist," *Lippincott's Magazine of Literature, Science, and Education* 1 (May 1868): 488. Rothermel likewise admired Neagle's art: he said of one of Neagle's portraits that it was "one of the finest heads ever painted. Stick a pin in that cheek and it will bleed" (p. 486).

17 Also in 1844 he married Caroline Goodhart, with whom he was to have three children: Blanche, John, and Peter Jr.

18 In the classes "under the careful and judicious supervision of MR. ROTHERMEL, who has voluntarily undertaken, on behalf of the Directors, the principal charge of this department, it is believed that essential advantages have accrued" (*Proceedings of the Annual Meeting of the Stockholders, June 4, 1855* [Philadelphia: Pennsylvania Academy of the Fine Arts, 1855], p. 10). Earlier, in 1852, along with Charles Macalester, Matthias W. Baldwin, and Henry D. Gilpin, Rothermel had urged the academy to expand to include "a Gallery of Free Exhibition (except at certain times), School of Instruction and a place for the deposit, distribution and sale of original works of art" (Minutes, February 14, 1852, p. 348, Archives, Pennsylvania Academy of the Fine Arts).

19 Ronald J. Onorato, "The Pennsylvania Academy of the Fine Arts and the Development of an Academic Curriculum in the Nineteenth Century," Ph.D. diss., Brown University, p. 58.

20 Ruoff, *Biographical and Portrait Cyclopedia*, p. 579. Ruoff was describing the life class begun in 1856.

[21] "Notices of Arts and Artists," *Sartain's Union Magazine of Literature and Art* 4 (June 1849): 44.

[22] "The Illustrations," *Bulletin of the American Art-Union* 6 (September 1, 1851): 85; the work was engraved by Alfred Jones for the Art-Union and appeared as the frontispiece of the issue. Another reproduction appeared in a gift book, *Ornaments of Memory* (1856).

[23] "Fine Arts," *Albion*, April 19, 1851, p. 189.

[24] "The Fine Arts," *Graham's Magazine* 37 (September 1850): 193–94. The writer also praised the painting's "exquisite qualities of color."

[25] "Fine Arts," *Albion*, May 17, 1851, p. 237. The writer was disagreeing with comments published in the New York *Evening Post*. English noted that "a keen stroke of satire appears on the right of the picture," where a famished woman with a sickly child "is in the full view of the zealots, who, in their zeal to uphold their religion, forget its loveliest attributes." (English, "Peter F. Rothermel," p. 16). For interpretations of the painting, see Wendy Greenhouse, "The American Portrayal of Tudor and Stuart History, 1835–1865," Ph.D. diss. Yale University, 1989, 1:220–38 and Gail E. Husch, " 'Something Coming': Prophecy and American Painting, 1848–1854," Ph.D. diss., University of Delaware, 1992, 1:311–13.

[26] Joseph Sill informed Rothermel that it had gone for only $675 and tried to allay the artist's disappointment by suggesting that the "large size [7 1/2 by 5 feet] was an objection to many, as it was difficult to find a place for so large a work in a modern Drawing Room" (December 17, 1852, Joseph Sill Diary, 10:194, Historical Society of Pennsylvania, [hereafter cited as HSP]). Rothermel had painted the work for John Towne for a $1000. Towne liked it but suggested to the artist that it might enhance his reputation if he sold it to the American Art-Union. When the Art-Union offered $800, Rothermel initially refused, then accepted (though still urging the Art-Union to "advance the matter of Price to the $1000"); see Rothermel to John Ridnor, July 1, 1851; Rothermel to Andrew Warner, July 1, 13, and 21, 1851, Letters from Artists, American Art-Union File, New-York Historical Society). Given that the work was originally valued at $1000, we can easily understand his frustration when the painting sold for $675 on December 16, 1852.

[27] English, "Peter F. Rothermel," p.16. The painting measured 5 x 4 feet. Other descriptions of the work, at some slight variance with English's, are found in: November 26, 1850, Joseph Sill Diary, 9:254–55, HSP: "Rothermel's Last Picture," *Philadelphia Art Union Reporter* 1 (January 1851): 19; Senior, "A Poem, a Prophecy, and a Picture," *Pennsylvania Freeman* (Philadelphia), March 13, 1851, p. 4 (originally published in Philadelphia's *New Era*, February, 1851, p. 1); and William F. Small, "Rothermel's Apotheosis of Labour; Or, 'The Labourer's Vision of Human Progress,' " *Sartain's Union Magazine of Literature and Art* 8 (April 1851): 277–79. (Small states the description is "copied from the Philadelphia Ledger of the 5th Feb.") Gail Husch offers an extended discussion of the work in regard to millenialism in her dissertation, " 'Something Coming,' " pp. 287–311, and includes a reconstructive drawing that she commissioned.

[28] Joseph Belcher, "Life and Writings of John Bunyan," *Sartain's Union Magazine of Literature and Art* 8 (March 1851): 190; Small, "Rothermel's Apotheosis of Labour," p. 277.

[29] Elizabeth M. Geffen, "William Henry Furness, Philadelphia Antislavery Preacher," *Pennsylvania Magazine of History and Biography* 82 (July 1958): 284–85. Years later, Furness presided over Rothermel's funeral services.

[30] English, "Peter F. Rothermel," p. 13, 16.

[31] Clipping from *Inquirer*, August 17, 1895, Scrapbooks of Thomas Hovenden. This article indicates that many of his biblical scenes also graced American homes.

[32] Lambdin had earlier moved that the president of the Pennsylvania Academy of the Fine Arts "memorialize Congress or take other measures that he may deem expedient with reference to one of the number of paintings that may be required to fill the pannels in the enlarged Capitol at Washington and that our townsman Mr. Rothermel be recommended to be employed in the premises" (Minutes, April 12, 1852, p. 339).

[33] "Petition of Thos Sully & others artists of Philada praying that Peter F. Rothermel may be employed to execute a historical painting for one of the public buildings in Washington," 32d Congress, Committee of the Library: Petitions and Memorials Series, National Archives, Washington, D.C.

[34] *The Congressional Globe: New Series: Containing the Debates, Proceedings, and Laws of the First Session of the Thirty-Second Congress* (Washington, D.C.: John C. Rives, 1852), 24:1321. On April 8 Cooper introduced a resolution that G. P. A. Healy and Emanuel Leutze be commissioned to execute paintings for the new Senate and House chambers. Each artist was to paint two subjects from the Revolutionary War (p. 1005). On May 11, Cooper indicated to Congress he was going to add Rothermel to the resolution.

[35] The June 8 resolution amended that of April 8, Cooper's new proposal asked that the three artists be commissioned to create two paintings each (*Congressional Globe*, 24:1533).

[36] M. C. Meigs to G[ouverneur] Kemble, February 8, 1854, as cited in Charles E. Fairman, *Art and Artists of the Capitol of the United States of America*, 69th Congress, 1st Sess., Senate Doc. 95 (Washington, D.C.: United States Government Printing Office, 1927), p. 149. Kemble's letter had praised Rothermel's painting "for truth and expression, and good color, [which] is equal to any thing that the other [Leutze] has done, and the drawing is better than in most of Leutze's pictures" (Kemble to Meigs, February 3, 1854, Curator of the Architect's Office, United States Capitol, Washington, D.C.)

[37] E. Digby Baltzell, *Philadelphia Gentleman: The Making of a National Upper Class* (Glencoe, Ill.: Free Press, 1958), p. 345. The Union League was founded in 1862.

[38] *Chronicle of the Union League of Philadelphia* (Philadelphia: Union League, 1902), p. 23.

[39] For a detailed account of this fascinating document, see Elizabeth M. Geffen, "Joseph Sill and His Diary," *Pennsylvania Magazine of History and Biography* 94 (July 1970): 275–330.

[40] April 27, 1841, Joseph Sill Diary, 3:15–17, HSP.

[41] May 19–21, 1851, Joseph Sill Diary, 9:358–59, HSP.

[42] April 21, September 5, 1852, Joseph Sill Diary, 10:41, 129, HSP.

[43] The unpaginated Rothermel notebook belongs to an individual who grew up in Linfield, Pa. (where Rothermel lived out his final years), and who generously made it available to me. Speaking of these commissions years later, Rothermel said that James Claghorn, President of the Pennsylvania Academy of the Fine Arts, on hearing that he was intent on paying his own way to Europe, asked if the artist would take commissions. "I did not object, but I told him I could go on my own hook. However, he sent me a letter with twenty names on it, commissioning me to paint pictures" ("A Venerable Artist," *Public Ledger*, p. 1). In the notebook, 19 names are listed on one page and 3 more on the following page.

[44] Rothermel also mentioned these in a later interview, where he indicated that Helena was sister to Emperor Nicholas, and that the prince was in attendance to the duchess; see "A Venerable Artist," *Public Ledger*, p. 1. The count's name also appears in the literature as "Kushelef" and "Konchileffde Besberodko" and the prince's as "Kotchabey."

[45] "Foreign Correspondence, Items, etc.," *Crayon* 5 (June 1858): 170; "Sketchings: Domestic Art Gossip," *Crayon* 5 (December 1858): 353.

[46] Entry of May 11, 1858, Rothermel notebook. Vansyckle sometimes appears as "Vansyckel."

[47] A detailed account of his experiences in London appears in a letter Rothermel wrote to James L. Claghorn August 30, 1856, Joseph Downs Collection of Manuscripts and Printed Ephemera, Library, Winterthur.

[48] Andrea Henderson notes the remarkableness of this group in Marc Simpson, et al., *Expressions of Place: The Art of William Stanley Haseltine* (San Francisco: Fine Arts Museum of San Francisco, 1992), p. 47 n. 24. Ila Weiss, *Poetic Landscapes: The Art and Experience of Sanford R. Gifford* (Newark: University of Delaware Press, 1987), p. 77.

[49] "A Venerable Artist," *Public Ledger*, p. 3.

[50] Rothermel to Joseph Patterson, October 7, 1857, Joseph Downs Collection of Manuscripts and Printed Ephemera, Library, Winterthur. This letter includes a lengthy discussion of Genazzano and its environs in the hills east of Rome.

[51] The paintings were *Saint Agnes*, *The Giants' Staircase*, and *The Virtuoso*. According to a newspaper account, although still unfinished "the force of the drawing and coloring were so conspicuous as to merit a special mention" ("Affairs at Paris," *New-York Daily Tribune*, August 4, 1859, p. 1). This report was cited in "American Art Abroad," *Cosmopolitan Art Journal* 3 (September 1859): 179. *Saint Agnes* is probably the composition shown at the Buffalo Fine Arts Academy that was listed as a "study" for Count Konchileffde Besberodko's large picture. *The Virtuoso* must have been a replica of the count's painting, which itself may have replicated a painting of the same title executed in 1853. One version is currently in the Museum of American Art of the Pennsylvania Academy of the Fine Arts. In a December 12, 1859, letter to her sister-in-law Ann Boswell Gratz, Rebecca Gratz noted that Rothermel had risen to great fame as an artist and that *The Giants' Staircase* had sold recently at auction for $980 (David Philipson, *Letters of Rebecca Gratz* [Philadelphia: Jewish Publication Society of America, 1929], p. 414). Apparently, Rebecca Gratz had given her brother Benjamin a Rothermel painting.

[52] "Affairs at Paris," *New-York Daily Tribune*, p. 1.

[53] [Probably late spring 1859], Rothermel notebook.

[54] Edward Strahan [Earl Shinn], *The Masterpieces of the Centennial International Exhibition* (1876; reprint, New York: Garland Publishing, 1977), 1:149–150.

[55] [Probably late spring 1859], Rothermel notebook

[56] Nancy Mowll Mathews, *Cassatt and Her Circle: Selected Letters* (Abbeville Press: New York, 1984), p. 16. Mathews discusses the relationship between Haldeman and Cassatt and includes many letters from and to Eliza Haldeman in her book (pp. 22–69).

[57] Haldeman to Samuel Haldeman, February 16, 1863, Archives, Pennsylvania Academy of the Fine Arts. In 1868 her father became professor of Comparative Philology at University of Pennsylvania.

[58] Haldeman to S. Haldeman, February 16, 1863.

[59] Haldeman to S. Haldeman, February 16, 1863. In a letter of March 20, 1863, she notes that "the old gentleman is accessible to flatterring."

[60] Rothermel to Claghorn, August 30, 1856.

[61] Haldeman to S. Haldeman, February 26, 1863. Asphatum, a dark brown transparent oil color, was popular with nineteenth-century painters.

[62] Haldeman to S. Haldeman, February 26, 1863.

[63] Haldeman to S. Haldeman, April 24, 1868, as cited in Mathews, *Cassatt and Her Circle*, 51.

[64] "Hovenden and Rothermel," *Press*, August 17, 1895, p. 4.

[65] For a recent discussion of the Sanitary Commission and the Great Central Fair, see J. Matthew Gallman, *Mastering Wartime: A Social History of Philadelphia during the Civil War* (Cambridge: Cambridge University Press, 1990).

[66] "Our Own Great Central Fair," *Our Daily Fare*, June 17, 1864, p. 69.

[67] The work is discussed in Edwin B. Coddington, "Rothermel's Paintings of the Battle of Gettysburg," *Pennsylvania History* 27 (January 1960): 1–27; Donald A. Winer, "Rothermel's Battle of Gettysburg: A Victorian's Heroic View of the Civil War," *Nineteenth Century* 1 (Winter 1975): 6–10; Kent Ahrens, "Painting for Peer, Patron, and the Public," *Pennsylvania Heritage* 18 (Spring 1992): 24–31.

[68] "Hovenden and Rothermel," *Press*, p. 4.

[69] Rothermel to R. Shelton Mackenzie, January 15, 1872, Gratz Collection, Historical Society of Pennsylvania.

[70] Charles F. Briggs, "Centennial Paintings: The American Department," *Independent*, July 13, 1876, p. 4; S[usan] N. C[arter], "Paintings at the Centennial Exhibition," *Art Journal*, n.s. 2 (September 1876): 284; John V. Sears, "Art in Philadelphia," *Aldine* 8 (June 1876):196. Sears begins the article in an earlier issue of the journal and states: "A cosmopolitan friend once said to me: 'There are more pictures to the square mile in Philadelphia than any other place in the world.'…There are a great many pictures here—mostly bad" ("Art in Philadelphia, I.," *Aldine* 8 [April 1876]: 112).

[71] S[usan] N. C[arter], "Art at the Exhibition," *Appleton's Journal*, June 31, 1876, p. 726.

[72] Clarence Cook, "A Centennial Blunder," *New-York Tribune*, May 4, 1876, p. 2. In this same letter to the editor, Cook claims "Mr. Rothermel is very much admired by a very few people in Philadelphia."

[73] Joaquin Miller, "The Great Centennial Fair and Its Future," *Independent*, July 13, 1876, p. 1.

[74] "The Fine Arts," *Independent*, May 18, 1876, p. 4. "Modern Art and Art Critics," *Potter's American Monthly* 7 (September 1876): 228.

[75] W[illiam] D[ean] Howells, "A Sennight of the Centennial," *Atlantic Monthly* 38 (July 1876): 94.

[76] Aside from the large battle picture, the London exhibition included the four smaller companion paintings plus *Christian Martyrs in the Coliseum*, *Hypatia*, *Bacchantes*, and *Lady Dedlock Leaving Tulkinghorn*.

[77] John Sartain, *The Reminiscences of a Very Old Man, 1808–1897* (New York: D. Appleton, 1899), p. 255.

[78] L., "Art—Philadelphia Art Notes," *Round Table*, June 25, 1864, p. 27.

[79] "The Claghorn Collection of Paintings," New York *Evening Post*, April 9, 1877, "Newspaper Clippings" book, p. 58, Papers of James Lawrence Claghorn, Archives of American Art, Smithsonian Institution. Rothermel's painting (unlocated today) takes as its source a passage from Thomas Buchanan Read's long, romantic poem of 1855, "House by the Sea": "Low at her feet pale Roland sat/Gazing up in her radiant face,/And said,' In such a time and place/How sweet were song, did thy voice but grace/The air with melody' " (*The Catalogue for the Thirty-Seventh Annual Exhibition of the Pennsylvania Academy of the Fine Arts* [Philadelphia, 1860], no. 307).

[80] "Fine Arts—Catalogue of the Art Collection of the Cincinnati Exposition," unidentified clipping [possibly from *New-York Tribune*], "Newspaper Clippings" book, p. 7, Papers of James Lawrence Claghorn. The Cincinnati exposition took place in 1873, and the work was listed as for sale. When shown at the Artists' Fund Society in New York in 1865, it was owned by S. P. Avery. At the centennial exhibition, Rothermel was listed as the owner, and the painting carried a descriptive subtitle, *Hypatia: The Neo-Platonic Philosopher Stripped and Torn to Pieces by the Christian Mob of Alexandria*. The painting is unlocated.

[81] Concerning this shift, see Mark Thistlethwaite, "A Fall from Grace: The Critical Reception of History Painting, 1875–1925," in William Ayres, ed., *Picturing History: American History Painting 1770–1930* (New York: Rizzoli, 1993), pp. 177–199.

[82] "The Fine Arts," *Evening Telegraph* (Philadelphia), December 17, 1870, Rothermel Papers, Pennsylvania State Archives, Harrisburg.

[83] "Gettysburg's Painter," *Evening Star* (Philadelphia), March 20, 1890, p. 3.

[84] Smith to Rothermel, [probably March 26, 1890], Smith Family Papers.

[85] "P. F. Rothermel Dead," *Public Ledger*, August 16, 1895, p. 1.

[86] The funeral services were held at the home of Peter F. Rothermel, Jr., 2013 Walnut St., Philadelphia, and were conducted by William H. Furness, pastor emeritus of the First Unitarian Church. Artists John and Emily Sartain, Peter Moran, and Thomas Eakins were among those in attendance ("Artist Rothermel Died," *Reading Weekly Eagle*, p. 1).

[87] "P. F. Rothermel Dead," *Public Ledger*, p. 1.

[88] "Sartain Talks of the Dead Artists," *Press*, p. 7.

[89] "Another Artist Passes Away," *Press*, p. 1.

Chronology

1812	July 8, born to John and Catherine Rothermel in Nescopeck, Luzerne County, Pennsylvania
ca. 1832	Moves to Philadelphia
ca. 1837	Studies with John Rubens Smith and Bass Otis
1838	Studio at 3rd and Callowhill Streets Exhibits first painting, *Portrait of a Gentleman,* with the Artists' Fund Society Elected member of Artists' Fund Society
1839	Becomes a member of the Board of Control of the Artists' Fund Society (serves through 1845)
1840	Studio at 14 N. 9th Street. Elected to the Council of the Artists' Fund Society (serves through 1843). Serves on education committee of Artists' Fund Society
1841	Journeys to the West with John Frankenstein; ends trip in Bedford, Pennsylvania, and returns to Philadelphia Studio at 86 Chestnut Street Serves on exhibition committee of the Artists' Fund Society Serves on annual report committee of the Artists' Fund Society
1842	Studio at 8 E. 6th Street
1844	Marries Caroline Goodhart, in Central Presbyterian Church, Philadelphia Studio at 16 Sansom Street Elected vice president of the Artists' Fund Society (serves through 1845)
1845	Daughter Blanche born
ca. 1845	Moves family to 2020 Race Street
1846	Elected to Board of Directors of the Pennsylvania Academy of the Fine Arts (serves through 1855) Studio at 16 Sansom Street
1847	Elected honorary member of the National Academy of Design Son John born
1849	Elected president of the Graphic Club of Philadelphia
1850	Son Peter, Jr. born
1851	Studio at 244 N. 11th Street Chairs a group of thirty-two artists pledging support for the Art Union of Philadelphia
1853	On Executive Committee of the Art Union of Philadelphia (serves through 1854)
1854	Chairs Committee on Instruction, the Pennsylvania Academy of the Fine Arts
1855	Supervises courses of instruction at the Pennsylvania Academy of the Fine Arts

1856	In August sails to Europe
	Visits London, Paris, Belgium, Dusseldorf, Florence
1857	By May settles in Rome
	Spends summer in nearby Genazzano
	In November, attends in Rome a meeting of artists and other friends of the recently deceased sculptor Thomas Crawford
1858	Stays mainly in Rome and Genazzano
1859	Travels to Munich, Venice, Paris
	Three paintings included in the Paris Salon
	In July, returns to Philadelphia
1860	Elected Academician of the Pennsylvania Academy of the Fine Arts
	Elected member of the Historical Society of Pennsylvania
1863	Founding member of the Union League of Philadelphia
1864	Elected president of the Artists' Fund Society
	Chairs committee of Philadelphia artists involved with the Great Central Fair of the United States Sanitary Commission
1866	Elected President of the Council of Academicians of the Pennsylvania Academy of the Fine Arts (serves through 1867)
1867	Serves on Board of Control of the Artists' Fund Society
	Studio at 15th and Market Streets
1868	Signs a petition of Philadelphia Artists addressed to Pennsylvania State Senator David McConaughy concerning import duties on foreign artist supplies and materials
1870	Purchases Grassmere, in Limerick, Montgomery County, as a summer home
1872	Becomes member of the Philadelphia Sketch Club
	Elected member of the American Philosophical Society
	Serves on Works of Art committee of the Fairmount Park Association
1875	Honored, along with Daniel Ridgeway Knight, James Hamilton, and F. O. C. Darley, with a reception at the Philadelphia Sketch Club
1876	Serves on advisory committee to the Centennial Exhibition Department of Art
1877	Moves to Grasssmere permanently
1879	Becomes member of the Philadelphia Society of Arts
ca. 1885	Begins suffering from cataracts
1887	Works included in exhibition of American art at Earl's Court, London
1890	Retrospective exhibition at the Art Club of Philadelphia
1895	August 15 dies of necrosis at Grassmere

List of Known Oil Paintings by Peter F. Rothermel

Dates indicate when the work was executed or first exhibited. Most titles are as given in the exhibition catalogues. Current locations are provided in brackets.

ca. 1837
Self-Portrait [Robert Gordon Stewart]
1838
Portrait of a Gentleman
1840
Genevieve
The Indian Mother
Jealousy
Scene from Taming of the Shrew
The Upset
The Weary Traveller
1841
Death of Old Mortality
The Messenger
Portrait of a Gentleman
Portrait of a Gentleman
Portrait of a Lady and Child
Scene from Calavar
Scene from Lalla Rookh
1842
Columbus before the Queen
[National Museum of American Art]
Fancy Picture
The Filagree Worker—Vide—The Ancient Regime
The Hawking Party—a scene from the "Betrothed"
Portrait of a Gentleman
Portrait of a Gentleman
Portrait of a Lady
Portrait of a Lady
1843
De Soto Discovering the Mississippi [St. Bonaventure University, St. Bonaventure, N.Y.]
Family Group
Interview of Mordaunt Merton with Norma on the shore of the Green Lock
Library 64. The Page
The Novice
Portrait of a Girl
Viola Pisani in the Bastile
1844
Cortés's First View of Mexico [New-York Historical Society]
Embarkation of Columbus
The Man who fought on his own hook
Portrait of a Gentleman
Portrait of a Lady
A Sketch
1845
Abraham Casting Out Hagar and Ishmael [Museum of American Art of the Pennsylvania Academy of the Fine Arts]
The Palmer's Return (The Noble Morringer)

Portrait of a Gentleman
Portrait of a Gentleman
Portrait of a Lady
Portrait of a Lady
Prayer of Tobit
Ruth and Boaz
Mrs. Shubrick protecting an American Soldier
The Surrender of Guatemozin [Kennedy Galleries, Inc., New York]
Washington prescribing for the poor Widow
1846
Cortés before Tenochtitlan [Cortés's Invasion of Mexico] [Lowe Art Museum, University of Miami]
Cortés Burning His Ships before Marching on Mexico [destroyed]
1847
Francis I. leaving his sons as hostages with the Emperor Charles V
Froissart Reading his Chronicles to Queen Phillipa
A Fugitive Cavalier after Defeat
King John accused of the Murder of Prince Arthur
Ruth and Naomi
1848
Cortez. Launch of the Brigantines "Noche Triste"
Ruth and Boaz
Showing Him the Way [Christie's 1993]
Washington the Evening before his Death
1849
Fanny Kemble
Judgment Scene in the Merchant of Venice
Lucy Ashton and Ravenswood at the Spring
Portrait of a Lady
1850
Banishment of Roger Williams [Rhode Island Historical Society, Providence]
Cromwell and Hitch, in Ely Cathedral [Cromwell Breaking Up the Service in an English Church]
First New England Sabbath [Mayflower Society, Plymouth]
Midsummer-night's Dream (Act IV, sc. 1)
Murray's Defence of Toleration
1851
De Soto Raising the Cross on the Banks of the Mississippi [Museum of American Art of the Pennsylvania Academy of the Fine Arts]
The Laborer's Vision of Human Progress
Lear and Cordelia [King Lear and

his Daughter] [private collection]
Memory
Origin of the Reformation
Patrick Henry in the House of Burgesses of Virginia, Delivering His Celebrated Speech against the Stamp Act [The Patrick Henry Memorial Foundation, Brookneal, Virginia]
Widow at the Tomb of Her Husband
1853
Antonio's Letter [Bassiano reading Antonio's Letter]
Banditti Robbing a Monastery
John Balfour of Burley in the Cave
David Playing the Harp before Saul [Philadelphia Museum of Art]
The Homeless
Milton and His Daughters [Harry Ransom Humanities Research Center, University of Texas at Austin]
Portrait of a Boy
Prejudice and Ill-will throwing dirt on the Garments of Innocence
Trial of Sir Henry Vane for High Treason
The Virtuoso [Museum of American Art of the Pennsylvania Academy of the Fine Arts]
1854
Cotter's Saturday Night
Cupid and Psyche
Landscape, with the story of Cimon and Iphigenia
Landing of the Pilgrims [Kirby Collection, Lafayette College, Easton, Pennsylvania]
Dr. H. S. Patterson (deceased)
The Penitent
Portrait of Dr. Elwood Harvey, Prof. of Principles and Practice of Medicine in the Female Medical College
Thou Art the Man [Museum of American Art of the Pennsylvania Academy of the Fine Arts]
Sir Walter Raleigh and Queen Elizabeth [private collection]
1855
Rose Bradwardine
A Country Girl
Judgment of Solomon
L'Amour
Portrait of a Child
Portrait of a Gentleman
Portrait of a Gentleman
Portrait of a Gentleman
Portrait of a Gentleman
Portrait of a Lady
Wood Nymph

1856
Edwin Forrest as King Lear [The
Actors' Home of the Actors'
Fund Englewood, N.J.]
Head of a Child
Lear and Cordelia (last act)
Portrait of a Child
Portrait of a Gentleman
Scene from "As You Like It"
1857
Little Bob
1858
King Lear [Schwarz Gallery,
Philadelphia]
Rubens and Van Dyck
Saint Agnes
The Three Marys at the Sepulchre
Too Tired to Play
1859
Abdication of Mary, Queen of Scots
*Benedict and Beatrice, from
Shakespeare's Comedy of Much
Ado About Nothing*
The Stairs of the Giants, at Venice
1860
Bianca Capelli
Coriolanus at the Gates of Rome
[Bowdoin College Art Museum]
*The House by the Sea [Roland and
Agatha]*
*"Landsknecht, Die," or Soldier Off
Guard*
*Last Moments of the Doge Francesco
Foscari*
Tasso and Leonora D'Este
Tired Love
1861
Christ and the Doctors [Reading
Public Museum, Reading,
Pennsylvania]
Col. C. G. Childs
*First Reading of the Declaration of
Independence* [Union League of
Philadelphia]
Magdalen
Napoleon at Moscow
Nunna. A Scene in Rome
Studio at Genazzano
1862
Christian Martyrs in the Coliseum
Exhausted Cupid [same as *Tired
Love?*]
Dr. Robert Shelton Mackenzie
[Historical Society of
Pennsylvania]
Portrait of a Gentleman
*State House, Day of the Battle of
Germantown* [Museum of American Art
of the Pennsylvania
Academy of the Fine Arts]
*Study for a Child in Christian
Martyrs* [Bowdoin College Museum
of Art]
Study of a Head of a Martyr
[Museum of American Art of
the Pennsylvania Academy of
the Fine Arts]
Anthony Wayne [Historical Society
of Pennsylvania]
1863
*Jeannie Deans and Madge Wildfire at
the Church Porch of Carlise*

Portrait of a Child
*Queen Elizabeth Signing the Death
Warrant of the Earl of Essex*
Romantic Landscape with Figures
Venezia
1864
Beggar Girl
Charity
Franklin at Versailles
Infant Bacchus
Last Sigh of the Moor [Museum of
American Art of the
Pennsylvania Academy of the
Fine Arts]
"Look at Dolly" [Historical
Society of Delaware]
Paul before Agrippa (and Festus)
Paul before Felix
The Soldier's Widow
1865
The Bather [Museum of American
Art of the Pennsylvania
Academy of the Fine Arts]
The Bather [private collection]
Desdemona [Museum of American
Art of the Pennsylvania
Academy of the Fine Arts]
Domenica
Hamlet and Ophelia
Hypatia
Italian Girl
Lady Macbeth
The Lay of the Last Minstrel
*Origin of the Guelph and Ghibelline
War*
Paul Preaching at Athens
Pleasure and Duty
Trajan and the Rabbi
1866
Desdemona [private collection]
Shylock and Jessica
1867
*Republican Court in the Days of
Lincoln* [The White House,
Washington, D.C.]

Sharpshooters at Round Top [State
Museum of Pennsylvania,
Harrisburg]
1868
*Queen Elizabeth at Kenilworth
Castle—Leicester Acknowledges his
Marriage with Amy Robsart*
1870
Bacchus, A Little Overcome
*The Battle of Gettysburg: Pickett's
Charge* [State Museum of
Pennsylvania, Harrisburg]
Cupid Reposing [private
collection]
The Little Irish Girl [Sotheby's,
1993]
Perdita, Winter's Tale
1872
Charge of the Pennsylvania Reserves
[State Museum of
Pennsylvania]
The Death of General Reynolds
[State Museum of
Pennsylvania]
Paul at Ephesus [Museum of
American Art of the

Pennsylvania Academy of the
Fine Arts]
*The Repulse of General Johnson's
Division* [State Museum of
Pennsylvania]
The Repulse of the Louisiana Tigers
[State Museum of
Pennsylvania]
1873
The Bride of Lammermoor
[Woodmere Art Museum,
Philadelphia]
1874
David Miller
Amy Robsart Interceding for Leicester
[private collection]
1876
Landscape near Limerick
*Macbeth Meditating the Murder of
Duncan*
Puck
1878
Richelieu
1879
Homer Reciting His Poetry
Hector Parting with Andromache
1880
Touchstone and Audrey
Bacchantes
1884
Lady Dedlock Leaving Tulkinghorn
[Raymond and Diane Waltz]

Undated
Sarah Tyndale Mitchell,
ca. 1840–1845
[private collection]
Sharon Tyndale, ca. 1840–1845
[private collection]
Annie Louisa and William Rank,
ca. 1844 [private collection]
Hagar and the Angel,
ca. 1845–1850
[private collection]
Portrait of an Unidentified Woman,
ca. 1855–1865 [Museum of
American Art of the
Pennsylvania Academy of the
Fine Arts]
Hector Tyndale, ca. 1863
[Historical Society of
Pennsylvania]
*Study for the Battle of Gettysburg:
Pickett's Charge,* ca. 1867–1870
[Museum of Fine Arts, Boston]
*Study for the Battle of Gettysburg:
Pickett's Charge,* ca. 1867–1870
[private collection]
Garden Scene
Massacre of the Silician Vespers
Ophelia Mad
Parting of the Knights of Tochenberg
The Rescue
Revolutionary Soldier on Black Stallion

Attributed to Rothermel
Children at the Well (or Pump) 1843 [Rifkin
Gallery, Riverdale, New York]
*Joseph Interpreting the Dreams of the Butler
and the Baker* [Museum of Art, Rhode
Island School of Design]

Catalogue of The Exhibition

(cat. 17) Detail of *First Reading of the Declaration of Independence,* 1861, oil on canvas, 41½ × 67½ in. Union League of Philadelphia

Self-Portrait

Cat. 1
Self-Portrait
ca. 1837
Oil on embossed cardboard,
6 × 4½ inches
(15.2 × 11.4 cm)
Robert Gordon Stewart

Fig. 6. *Mr. Rothermel at 21.* Photograph from *The Philadelphia Times,* August 16, 1895, 3. Courtesy of the Montgomery County Historical Society

Written on the mat is "Rothermell." Although not in the artist's hand, this inscription identifies both the artist and the sitter. This small oval image is a Rothermel self-portrait.

The work resembles both the image that appeared with Thomas Dunn English's 1852 article and the representation of the artist at age twenty-one accompanying his obituary in the *Philadelphia Times* (figs. 4 and 6). All three likenesses present a man with similarly shaped and sized eyes, nose, and lips. Another work, Jeremy Wilson's 1858 depiction of Rothermel at his easel (fig. 7), also shows features similar to those in the oval painting, especially the unkempt "artistic" hair. That mop of hair also distinguishes the artist standing before an easel in a drawing by Rothermel, inscribed "Artist Studio/P. F. Rothermel," which shows sharper facial features, is also a plausible self-portrait (fig. 7). A fifth and final image that supports the designation of the small oval as a self-portrait is a photograph of Rothermel taken late in life (see fig. 1). Although decades separate the two likenesses, it is possible to see the features of the young man maturing into those of "this Patriach among painters."[1]

In addition to the visual evidence, the small size of the circa 1837 oval portrait reinforces its attribution to the youthful Rothermel. Rothermel was then either studying under Bass Otis or commencing his career as a portraitist. Whichever the case, the creation of a small self-portrait by a young artist with little money for supplies or models and few works to show prospective clients would be logical and expedient.

[1] "A Venerable Artist," *Public Ledger,* March 19, 1890, p. 3.

Fig. 7. Jeremy Wilson, *Rothermel at his Easel, 1858.* Unlocated

Fig. 8 [cat. 51] *"The Artist's Studio,"* ca. 1850–1853. Gil. E. Pablo. M.D. Collection

35

Columbus before the Queen

Cat. 2
Columbus before the Queen
1841–1842
Oil on canvas,
62 3/8 × 50 inches
(158.4 × 127 cm)
National Museum of American
Art, Smithsonian Institution

This romantic composition is Rothermel's first grand history painting. In 1841 a writer reported:

> ROTHERMEL is at present engaged in painting a large picture, on a national subject—COLUMBUS BEFORE THE QUEEN. It is the largest, and promises to be by far the most brilliant and beautiful, of all the historical subjects which have proceeded from the prolific pencil of this gifted artist. The design is quite simple; the figures few: but for freedom, breadth, and expression, it may already be pronounced admirable. It is Mr. Rothermel's intention to introduce the picture into the Artists' Fund Exhibition; it will be one of the best pictures in the exhibition.[1]

Columbus before the Queen did indeed appear in the Artists' Fund Society exhibition of 1842.[2] The following year it formed part the organization's special exhibition, where it was listed as belonging to Philadelphia banker Edward S. Whelan.[3] Another Rothermel depiction of the navigator, *Embarkation of Columbus* (unlocated), appeared in the society's 1844 exhibition.[4] Its catalogue entry includes a passage from Washington Irving's *History of the Life and Voyages of Christopher Columbus* (1828), a popular book that in all likelihood had also inspired *Columbus before the Queen*.

Rothermel's rendering captures the spirit of Irving's writing, which characterizes Isabella as "one of the purest and most beautiful characters on the pages of history" and asserts that Columbus's vision suddenly "broke upon her mind in its real grandeur."[5] In addition to Irving, the artist likely consulted William Prescott's history of Ferdinand and Isabella. Prescott particularly emphasized Isabella's role in supporting Columbus's venture:

> We must remember…[that] she did in fact furnish the resources essential to its execution; that she undertook the enterprise when it had been explicitly declined by other powers, and when probably none other of that age would have been found to countenance it; and that, after once plighting her faith to Columbus, she became his steady friend, shielding him against the calumnies of his enemies, reposing in him the most generous confidence, and serving him in the most acceptable manner, by supplying ample resources for the prosecution of his glorious discoveries.[6]

Compositionally, *Columbus before the Queen* features elements that Rothermel later used in a number of paintings, including *Patrick Henry in the Virginia House of Burgesses, Delivering His Celebrated Speech against the Stamp Act* (cat. 8) and *Thou Art the Man* (cat. 11)—a confrontation between a lone hero and an elevated authority, a crowd displaying a variety of reactions, a scribe who has paused in his writing, a figure who stills another, and imposing architecture.

Rothermel clothed the Genoese navigator in elegant, but historically

inaccurate, garb. At the hero's feet lie books (one inscribed "Marco Polo," an explorer Irving cited as influencing Columbus), maps, and a terrestial globe. The picture portrays Columbus as a learned, aristocratic explorer. On a dais sits the king, while the queen stands transfixed with her crossed hands pressing against her bejeweled necklace, a gesture that evokes the legend of Isabella offering her jewelry to finance the voyage. Isabella's saintly demeanor ("she was filled with a pious zeal at the idea of effecting such a great work of salvation"), the reverent attitude of her seated attendant, the trumpeting sculptural figure high above Columbus's head, and the misty Gothic interior imbue the scene with a religious aura. This is enhanced by the rose lying on the pavement, a flower that carries many Christian connotations, including that of heavenly joy. Taking his cue from Irving, Rothermel suggested the missionary dimensions of Columbus's vision: "A deep religious sentiment mingled with his mediations, and gave them at times a tinge of superstition, but it was of a sublime and lofty kind. He looked upon himself as standing in the hand of heaven, chosen from among men for the accomplishment of its high purpose."[7]

Shaped as it was by popular historical writings, Rothermel's *Columbus before the Queen* imparts the elevated, romantic view of the hero that Americans embraced on the 350th anniversary of his "discovery."[8]

[1] "Painting," *Young People's Book* 2 (1841): 78. This journal was edited by John Frost, "professor of Belles Lettres, Philadelphia High School."

[2] *Columbus Relating His Discoveries to Ferdinand and Isabella* exhibited at the Boston Athenaeum (and offered for sale) later in 1842, is, presumably, *Columbus before the Queen* with a variant title.

[3] In the catalogue "Wheelan" is the spelling. A 1976 letter in the National Museum of American Art files states that according to family tradition Whelen commissioned the work; however, no owner is listed in the Artists' Fund Society catalogue, and the Boston Athenaeum catalogue later that year indicates the picture, which I take to be the same one, was for sale.

[4] *Embarkation of Columbus* was presented to the Pennsylvania Academy of the Fine Arts in 1844 by its president, Joseph Dugan, and was sold at auction in 1898.

[5] Washington Irving, *Life and Voyages of Christopher Columbus*, ed. John Harmon McElroy (Boston: Twayne Publishers, 1981), pp. 43, 65.

[6] William H. Prescott, *History of the Reign of Ferdinand and Isabella* (3d ed.; New York: American Publishers Association, 1838), 1:350–51.

[7] Irving, *Life and Voyages of Christopher Columbus*, pp. 68, 30.

[8] Columbus subjects were popular in Europe and the United States at the time. Paintings from the 1840s include Robert Weir's *Columbus before the Council of Salamanca* (1841); Emanuel Leutze's *Columbus before the Council of Salamanca* (1841), *The Return of Columbus in Chains to Cadiz* (1842), and *Columbus before the Queen* (1843); Asher B. Durand's *The Embarkation of Columbus* (ca. 1843); Abraham Woodside's *Return of Columbus* (1845), *Columbus at the Court of Ferdinand and Isabella* (1846), and *Queen Anacona Taken Captive* (1847); William Powell's *Columbus before the Council of Salamanca* (1847); John Vanderlyn's *The Landing of Columbus* (finished and installed in the Capitol Rotunda in 1847). For a consideration of Columbus depictions, see Jules David Prown, "Washington Irving's Interest in Art and His Influence upon American Painting," M.A. thesis, University of Delaware, 1956), pp. 69–133; A. D. Miles Hamish, "Wilkie's *Columbus*," *North Carolina Museum of Art Bulletin* 8 (March 1969): 3–15; and Ann Uhry Abrams, "Visions of Columbus: The 'Discovery' Legend in Antebellum American Paintings and Prints," *American Art Journal* 24 (1993): 75–101. For discussions of Rothermel's painting in context, see William H. Truettner, ed., *The West as American: Reinterpreting Images of the Frontier, 1820–1920* (Washington, D.C.: Smithsonian Institution Press, 1991), pp. 57–59, and Thomas J. Schlereth, "Columbia, Columbus, and Columbianism," *Journal of American History* 79 (December 1992): 937–68.

Annie Louisa and William Rank

Cat. 3
Annie Louisa and William Rank
c. 1844
Oil on canvas, 43 × 32 inches
(109.2 × 81.3 cm)
Private collection

While Peter Rothermel gained fame as a history painter, he was also executing a number of portraits. Indeed, he began his career as a portraitist: his first recorded exhibited work (1838) was *Portrait of a Gentleman,* and throughout the 1840s Philadelphia city directories listed him as a portrait painter. From 1838 to 1863 (when he virtually ceased exhibiting portraits), Rothermel showed approximately 36 portraits, which accounts for almost a quarter of the approximately 150 pictures he exhibited during this period. The majority of these portraits carried only generic titles, such as *Portrait of a Child, Portrait of a Lady,* and a survey of exhibition catalogues reveals that several of those who owned his portraits—including William D. Kelly, Matthias W. Baldwin, Joseph Patterson and Edward P. Mitchell—also purchased his history paintings.

In this early portrait, executed about the time he committed himself to history painting, Rothermel presents the children of Philadelphia dry goods merchant, Joseph Rank. Annie Louisa, age four, and her six-year-old brother William appear in an idealized environment.[1] With its distant landscape, elaborate urn, butterfly (signifying fleeting youth), flower (fertility), and book (knowledge), the painting embraces the style and symbolism of genteel portraiture well established by eighteenth century British artists. As such, the portrait represents an ambitious attempt by Rothermel to enter into that tradition. Like a number of his compositions, this one displays its affinity with the art of Thomas Sully, the English-born Philadelphia artist Rothermel admired.

[1] I am grateful to James L. Elson for bringing this portrait to my attention.

Cortés before Tenochtitlan [Cortés's Invasion of Mexico]

Cat. 4
Cortés before Tenochtitlan
[*Cortés's Invasion of Mexico*]
Inscribed lower right:
  P. F. Rothermel 1846
Oil on canvas,
37½ × 48 inches
(95.3 × 121.9 cm)
Lowe Art Museum, University
of Miami; Museum purchase
through Harry and Sonja
Zuckerman Funds

This is a version of the subject that in 1844 initiated Rothermel's series of five paintings depicting the exploits of Hernan Cortés. For inspiration, the artist turned to William Hickling Prescott's *History of the Conquest of Mexico* (1843) an immensely popular book:

As a piece of writing, the artistic excellence of the work challenges our highest admiration. In passages where the change became appropriate, the pen in the author's hand has become the historic pencil. The whole of the march to Mexico is full of paintings, warmly colored, but not exaggerated…[Prescott] has drawn a gorgeous picture of the valley…[with] hues of his own feelings.[1]

Prescott's sensibility fired the imagination of Rothermel, who, a contemporary noted,

seems to have a penchant for the heroic age of our western world—for we have had our age of chivalry as well as Europe. Columbus and Cortés and Soto, Rothermel's favourites, were all belted knights in their time—and knights errant, too, for they wandered further in quest of adventures than even the Crusaders.[2]

In *Cortés before Tenochtitlan*, Rothermel's "crusaders" stand in awe of the Aztec capital. The cactus in the foreground symbolizes the origin of Tenochtitlan, a name signifying, so Prescott had explained, "*tunal* (a cactus) *on a stone.*" The figures convey the conflicted reactions of the Spaniards to the spectacle that Prescott had described: "feelings of admiration were soon followed by others of a very different complexion; as they saw in all this the evidences of a civilization and power far superior to anything they had yet encountered." While the "sanguine spirit" of Cortés, who stands to the right of center above Marina, his mistress, experienced no intrepidation or melancholy, the overall composition does evoke a romantic broodiness.[3]

An 1852 article on Rothermel by Thomas Dunn English provides the best account of the patronage of the five Cortés pictures:

Professor Mapes, who has done so much to encourage art and artists in this country, saw while on a visit to Philadelphia, the picture of "Columbus before the Queen;" and, being struck with some of its points, left with a friend an order for Rothermel to paint one of the same size, sufferng the artist to choose the subject; and adding, that if, when finished, any one fancied it, the artist should sell the picture, and paint another instead. At that time Prescott's work on "The Conquest of Mexico" was making a great noise, and furnished a number of good subjects. Rothermel selected "Cortez haranguing his Troops, within sight of the Valley of Mexico," and painted, as he says, "a very fair picture." It was much more, however, than "very fair,"—being a glorious composition, remarkable for its vigor, force, and combination of fine tone with richness of colour. It attracted the attention of a liberal patron of the arts,

Warrington Gillette, of New York, but at that time a resident of Baltimore, who gave Rothermel without hesitation the price he demanded, and thus an invaluable addition to his own collection. Professor Mapes, saw the picture, liked it so much, that he ordered its substitute to be founded on a similar subject,—"The Surrender of Guatemozin." This, which was also an admirable specimen of drawing and colouring, was duly executed and delivered. These paintings attracted such admiration, that several more, on similar themes, were ordered. One of these "Noche Triste; or, The Morning of the Retreat on the Causeway,"—was for Mr. Binney, of Boston; another,—"Cortez Burning his Fleet,"—for James Robb, of New Orleans; a third,—"Launch of the Brigantines,"—for J. B. H. Latrobe, of Baltimore, son of the architect of the Capitol; and a fourth,—the subject unknown to me,—which is now in the possession of the artist's cousin, Samuel H. Rothermel, of Philadelphia.[4]

The patronage testifies to the artist's growing reputation and the interest his subject matter generated at midcentury.

This particular painting, dated 1846, is the second version of the subject, and is the one belonged to Rothermel's cousin Samuel in 1852. For many years it belonged to the Union League of Philadelphia, an organization whose members included both Samuel and Peter Rothermel. The first version, dated 1844, belongs to the New-York Historical Society, where it carries the title *Cortez's First View of Mexico City*. Although the two paintings are virtually identical in size, they differ significantly in composition and mood. The earlier painting shows Cortés haranguing his troops; the later version portrays him in a more introspective mood.

[1] G. T. C., "Prescott's Conquest of Mexico," *Christian Examiner* 36 (March 1844): 225–26. See also, Donald A. Ringe, "The Artistry of Prescott's 'The Conquest of Mexico,' " *New England Quarterly* 26 (December 1953): 454–76.

[2] An Amateur, "Visits to the Painters," *Godey's Lady's Book* 29 (December 1844): 277.

[3] William H. Prescott, *History of the Conquest of Mexico and History of the Conquest of Peru* (1843 and 1847; reprint, 2 vols in 1, New York: Modern Library, 1936), pp. 16, 287.

[4] Thomas Dunn English, "Peter F. Rothermel," *Sartain's Union Magazine of Literature and Art* 10 (January 1852): 15. *The Surrender of Guatemozin* is discussed on the following pages. *"Noche Triste"* was exhibited at Boston Athenaeum in 1848, and Mrs. A. Binney was listed as owner; it appeared there again in 1863 with a Mrs. Hayward named as owner. Dr. Amos Binney, a naturalist, had commissioned the work; he died in 1847. *Cortés Burning His Ships* (destroyed) was exhibited at Western Art-Union in 1849 and 1850, National Academy of Design in 1847, and Buffalo Fine Arts Academy in 1864 and 1866–69. Rothermel's May 26, 1846, letter to James Robb, a banker and president of the New Orleans Gas Light and Banking Co., describes the subject (Historic New Orleans Collection). Joseph Sill (May 18, 1846, Diary, 7: 74, Historical Society of Pennsylvania [hereafter cited as HSP]) deemed it an excellent work, but a critic assessed it a weak example of history painting ("The Fine Arts: Exhibition at the National Academy," *Literary World* [April 24, 1847]: 279). *Launch of the Brigantines* (unlocated) was shown at both the Pennsylvania Academy of the Fine Arts and the Maryland Historical Society in 1848. Earlier, *Godey's* had opined that it would add to the artist's reputation as a painter and "thinker" ("Notices of the Fine Arts," *Godey's Lady's Book* 35 [December 1847]: 328), and *Literary World* had termed the work "remarkable for its correct drawing and fidelity of character" ("The Fine Arts," *Literary World* [January 29, 1848], 632). In April 1848 *Godey's* again praised the still incomplete work for its "spirit and vivacity" ("Notices of the Fine Arts," *Godey's Lady's Book* 36 [April 1848]: 245). Five months later, when reviewing the Pennsylvania Academy exhibition, *Godey's* termed the work "charming" and added: "The painting is very faithful and carefully elaborated, the characters marked with great individuality—though bordering rather too closely upon the grotesque here and there—and the story well told" ("Notices of the Fine Arts," *Godey's Lady's Book* 37 [September 1848]: 176). English's text reversed the middle initials of lawyer John H. B. Latrobe, the painting's owner.

The Surrender of Guatemozin

Cat. 5
The Surrender of Guatemozin
Inscribed lower right:
  P. F. Rothermel / 1845
Oil on canvas, 37 1/2 × 49 inches
(95.3 × 124.5 cm)
Kennedy Galleries Inc.,
New York

On April 2, 1845, Joseph Sill visited Rothermel's studio, "but was sorry to find that he [the artist] had sent his best Picture of "The Interview between Cortes and the Mexican Monarch" to New York; and had sold it for $300—I wanted much to see this Picture, and will endeavour to do so when I go to New York."[1] The composition, more properly titled *The Surrender of Guatemozin*, was executed for Prof. James J. Mapes and is the second in the artist's series of paintings based on William Hickling Prescott's *History of the Conquest of Mexico*.[2]

[Cortés] then made preparations for the interview; caused the terrace to be carpeted with crimson cloth and matting, and a table to be spread with provisions, of which the unhappy Aztecs stood so much in need. His lovely Indian princess, Doña Marina, was present to act as interpreter. She had stood by his side through all the troubled scenes of the Conquest, and she was there now to witness its triumphant termination.

Guatemozin, on landing, was escorted by a company of infantry to the presence of the Spanish commander. He mounted the *azotea* with a calm and steady step, and was easily to be distinguished from his attendant nobles, though his full, dark eye was no longer lighted up with its accustomed fire, and his features wore an expression of passive resignation....

Cortés came forward with a dignified and studied courtesy to receive him. The [defeated] Aztec monarch...first broke the silence by saying; "I have done all that I could, to defend myself and my people. I am now reduced to this state. You will deal with me, Malinche, as you list."[3]

Like Rothermel's other history paintings, the composition brims with a variety of figures and attributes that telescope passages from its narrative source.[4] Rothermel included no table spread with provisions but did place Cortés's mistress (seated, however) next to him. The artist assigned Cortés a more expansive gesture of greeting than that suggested by Prescott, and Guatemozin's restrained stance—arms folded and feet shackled (which would have inhibited climbing the *azotea* with "a calm and steady step")—perhaps foreshadows his execution at Cortés's order.[5] Next to Guatemozin is his wife, Princess Tecuichpo (the daughter of Montezuma), who in the book appears after this confrontation. Cortés and his party stand beneath the fluttering banner of victorious Spain; Guatemozin and his wife stand against the smoke of defeat. For its original audience, *The Surrender of Guatemozin* suggested the conquest of the light of reason and faith over the darkness of savagery. Animated by the spirit of Manifest Destiny, Rothermel's contemporaries likely viewed this composition as western civilization triumphantly welcoming the "others" to its vision of a New World.

The work appeared in the National Academy of Design's annual exhibition in 1845. *Broadway Journal*, a publication admittedly biased against history and "ideal" paintings, gave a mixed review:

> [It is] by one of the most promising artists of the mob city; but not to our view one of his best pictures....There are some very pretty figures, but they appear like a group of fashionable ladies and gentlemen in a *tableau vivant*, rather than real personages in the drama of life.[6]

Criticism of this sort—centering on theatricality—continually plagued Rothermel and other history painters. The difficulty such artists faced was how to produce highly dramatic, narrative scenes without provoking charges of melodramatic excess.

[1] April 2, 1845, Joseph Sill Diary 6:172, HSP.

[2] Mapes "that generous, warm-hearted and discriminating patron of genius" ("Notices of Arts and Artists," *Sartain's Union Magazine of Literature and Art* 4 [June 1849]: 414), was an inventor and agricultural chemist who held the chair of chemistry and natural philosophy at the National Academy of Design, New York.

[3] William H. Prescott, *History of the Conquest of Mexico and History of the Conquest of Peru* (1843 and 1847; reprint, 2 vols in 1, New York: Modern Library, 1936), pp. 606–7. Much of this passage appeared in the catalogue entry for the painting at the Brooklyn Institute in October 1845; James L. Yarnall and William H. Gerdts, *The National Museum of American Art's Index to American Art Catalogues: From the Beginning through the 1876 Centennial Year* (Boston: G. K. Hall, 1986), 4:3060.

[4] For a discussion of compositional affinity between this painting and Diego Velázquez's *Surrender at Breda* (1634–35), see William H. Truettner, ed., *The West as America: Reinterpreting Images of the Frontier, 1820–1920* (Washington, D.C.: Smithsonian Institution Press, 1991), pp. 79–80.

[5] This observation was made by Katherine Moody, who helped me better understand this painting.

[6] "The National Academy," *Broadway Journal*, May 17, 1845, p. 307. The journal's comments the week before were even more negative. The appellation "mob city" derives from the riots in Philadelphia in 1844 and earlier.

(Cat. 6)

47

Hagar and the Angel

Cat. 6
Hagar and the Angel
ca. 1845–1850
Inscribed lower right:
  P. F. Rothermel / 18__ [illegible]
Oil on canvas,
25 ⅛ × 30 ¼ inches
(63.8 × 76.8 cm)
Henry and Pearl Gerlach
Collection

This painting stylistically resembles the artist's *Ruth and Boaz* of 1845 (cat. 35) and relates thematically to a picture he exhibited in 1845: *Abraham Casting Out Hagar and Ishmael* (Pennsylvania Academy of the Fine Arts), a copy of Guercino's well-known painting of 1657–58.[1]

Egyptian-born Hagar, servant to Sarai (wife of Abram and later called Sarah), had been given by Sarai to Abram (Abraham) so that a child might be conceived, after which Hagar looked with contempt on Sarai. In turn, Sarai dealt harshly with Hagar, who then fled:

> The angel of the LORD found her by a spring of water in the wilderness, the spring on the way to Shur. And he said, "Hagar, maid of Sarai, where have you come from and where are you going? she said, "I am fleeing from my mistress Sarai." The angel of the LORD said to her, "Return to your mistress, and submit to her." [Genesis 16:7–9.]

The gestures of Rothermel's angel in this portrayal convey both the questioning of Hagar and the command to return. In some nineteenth-century glosses on this biblical passage, the wandering Hagar is described as melancholic. Possibly that is her attitude here, where, lost in introspection, she is unaware of the substantial divine manifestation. What is unusual and problematic about Rothermel's depiction is the prominent staff with which Hagar inscribes the sand, an action not part of the subject's traditional iconography. The Hebrew word for "staff" is the same as that for "tribe," and the Bible does have the angel informing Hagar that her descendants (her tribe) will so multiply as to be countless. While this connection is certainly intriguing, whether Rothermel knew or meant this connection remains speculative. Other than the staff, the composition recognizably portrays the confrontation of the angel and Hagar.[2]

[1] The Guercino is in the Brera Art Gallery, Milan. When *Abraham Casting Out Hagar and Ishmael* was exhibited in the Rothermel exhibition at the Art Club of Philadelphia in 1890, the artist identified it as his first attempt at copying a European masterpiece (Registrar's Files, Pennsylvania Academy of the Fine Arts). Since that painting reverses Guercino's composition, Rothermel must have worked from a print. I appreciate Beverly Brown's assistance in establishing that many prints after Guercino's painting were available for Rothermel to copy.

[2] Claudia Camp, Sharon Gouwens, and David Gunn provided insightful comments as I tried to confirm the identification of the subject. All agreed that inclusion of the staff was unusual but that the subject's identity as Hagar and the angel was most plausible. It was Professor Camp who informed me of the connection between "staff" and "tribe." While no exhibition records cite a *Hagar and the Angel* by Rothermel, no titles of his unlocated exhibited works offer a more appropriate one.

De Soto Raising the Cross on the Banks of the Mississippi

Cat. 7
De Soto Raising the Cross on the Banks of the Mississippi
1851
Inscribed on canvas folded over stretcher:
  [Ro]thermel
Oil on canvas, 40 × 50 inches (101.6 × 127 cm)
Museum of American Art of the Pennsylvania Academy of the Fine Arts, Philadelphia; funds provided by the Henry C. Gibson Fund and Mrs. Elliott R. Detchon

This was Rothermel's second depiction of the life of Hernando de Soto. His earlier *De Soto Discovering the Mississippi* (see fig. 2), exhibited at the Artists' Fund Society in 1843, the National Academy of Design in 1844, and then purchased by the American Art-Union, was the first picture to draw widespread attention to Rothermel as a history painter. *De Soto Raising the Cross on the Banks of the Mississippi*, with its more complex composition and more fully realized forms, is an especially fine example of the artist's mature style.

This painting received notice in early 1852:

A SPLENDID PAINTING of "De Soto Raising the Cross on the Mississippi," (supposed to be the first religious service in America,) painted by Rothermel for the Western Art-Union, to be distributed, with other works of art, in March next, may be seen for a few days at Earle's Gallery, 216 Chestnut Street. The print for members will be "The Committee of Congress drafting the Declaration of Independence," a beautiful engraving from a painting by Rothermel [see cat. 35].[1]

The appearance of the artist's *Cortés Commanding the Burning of His Ships* (1846) at the Western Art-Union exhibition of 1849 may have led to the execution of *De Soto Raising the Cross*, for Western Art-Union pointedly encouraged American historical imagery:

The story of America has been well written by historians, but, it's true that lessons received by the eye are more impressive, more lasting....And might not this Society...do much for the honor of the country, and acquire a high position for itself, by becoming the pictorial illustrators of American History? The History of America recorded by the hands of her Artists![2]

In a dramatic scene, Rothermel conveyed the "naturalness" of planting Christianity in the New World. The primitive altar, constructed of a stump and cut limbs, stands under an arbor canopy. Nature shapes the holy event. The sturdy timber cross, rising above a dead tree, is rooted in the new Eden. One soldier straining to help elevate the cross pierces it in a manner recalling Longinus lancing Christ. Figures offer a variety of responses to the momentous occasion, including a prostrate Indian at the feet of the priest. The artist's

50

rendering of the contemplative de Soto and the Indian at left are especially rich in color and textures. Rothermel enlivens the scene with his vivid use of darks and lights, and enhances the action by moving the viewer's eye through the picture by touches of orangish red paint.

De Soto Raising the Cross, along with the earlier *De Soto Discovering the Mississippi*, is one of several of the artist's compositions depicting noted explorers, including Columbus and Cortés. Such subjects were popular among painters at midcentury and reflected both an interest in American history and an implicit connection to (and, perhaps, legitimization of) the expansionism inherent in the concept of Manifest Destiny.[3] Our presumption that Rothermel's painting tapped into the public's interest in the explorer is reinforced by another event—the staging of "The Tragedy of de Soto," at Philadelphia's Chestnut Steet Theatre in 1852.[4] Coincidentally, an actor, Edwin Forrest, once owned (and may have commissioned) this dramatic painting.[5]

[1] *North American and United States Gazette*, January 22, 1852, p. 2. Joseph Sill mentions that the painting was executed for the "Cincinnati Art Union" (December 21, 1851, Joseph Sill Diary, 9: 486, HSP). Since no record of a Cincinnati Art Union can be found, Sill may have meant the Western Art-Union; however, that organization disbanded in early 1851. Thus, the painting's connection to the Western Art-Union is problematic.

[2] *Transactions of the Western Art-Union, for the Year 1849* (Cincinnati, 1849), p. 15. This goal was repeated in the 1850 *Transactions*.

[3] For a detailed consideration of this topic, see William H. Truettner, "The Art of History: American Exploration and Discovery Scenes, 1840–1860," *American Art Journal* 14 (Winter 1982): 4–31.

[4] "The Tragedy of de Soto," *North American and United States Gazette*, April 22, 1852, p. [1]. The play's closing scene took the form of a tableaux vivant representing William Powell's picture of the burial of de Soto in the Mississippi. At this time, Powell was nearing completion of another de Soto painting: his depiction of the Spaniard's discovery of the Mississippi, for the United States Capitol Rotunda. The scenery for the play was painted by Rothermel's good friend, Russell Smith; see Virginia E. Lewis, *Russell Smith, Romantic Artist* (Pittsburgh: University of Pittsburgh Press, 1956), p. 190.

[5] Registrar's Files, Pennsylvania Academy of the Fine Arts.

Patrick Henry in the House of Burgesses of Virginia, Delivering His Celebrated Speech against the Stamp Act

Cat. 8
Patrick Henry in the House of Burgesses of Virginia, Delivering His Celebrated Speech against the Stamp Act
Inscribed lower right:
  P. F. Rothermel / 1851
Oil on canvas, 79 × 61 inches
(200.7 × 154.9 cm)
The Patrick Henry Memorial
Foundation, Brookneal, Virginia

Fig. 9 Robert Edge Pine. *Garrick Reciting an Ode to Shakespeare.* Stipple engraving by Caroline Watson. London, British Museum

This masterpiece is one of the major American paintings from the mid nineteenth century. The Philadelphia *Sun* termed it "the best historical painting ever executed in America,…[which] places the artist in the front rank of his profession among painters of the world."[1] *Graham's Magazine* declared, "[Rothermel] has thrown into it all the fire of his genius, all the ardor of his patriotism, all the accumulation of his knowledge and skill as one of the practiced and leading historical painters of the day."[2] Painted expressly for the Art Union of Philadelphia as its First Prize of 1852, the commission resulted from the Art Union's managers being "deeply impressed with utility, necessity, wisdom and moral influence of cherishing a national subject, in the patronage of the Arts of Design, in the United States, and a national pride in the excellence of her living Artists." The commissioning of this work also marked a change in policy for the Art Union, which, like its model, the London Art Union, had previously distributed, by lot, certificates with which paintings might be purchased. In 1851 the Philadelphia Art Union, announced that it planned to "procure annually, an original picture from one of the first living Artists of our Country, to be engraved for the subscribers of that year, and to be awarded as the highest prize at the annual Distribution."[3] That such a significant commission fell to Rothermel indicates his high reputation within the Philadelphia art community.[4]

The composition portrays the most dramatic moment in Henry's resolutions opposing the 1765 Stamp Act. The Virginian, in the stirring words of William Wirt, Henry's biographer,

> exclaimed in a voice of thunder, and with the look of a god, "Caesar had his Brutus—Charles the First, his Cromwell—and George the Third"— ("Treason," cried the speaker—"Treason, treason!" echoed from every part of the house.—It was one of those trying moments which is decisive of character—Henry faltered not an instant; but rising to a loftier attitude, and fixing on the speaker an eye of the most determined fire, he finished his sentence with the firmest emphasis) "*may profit by their example. If this be treason, make the most of it.*"[5]

This passage, which served as Rothermel's primary inspiration, often accompanied contemporary accounts of the painting.

Rothermel set the orator in a crowd-filled chamber of massive columns and sweeping forms. Space recedes sharply to emphasize the grandeur of the place and the dynamism of the moment. Patrick Henry, confronting the seated Speaker of the House, John Robinson, has just delivered his inflammatory words. Rothermel animated the crowd's reactions through gesture, body language, and facial expressions so that "every inch of the canvas tells the story. The spectator, who knew nothing of the scene or of its actors would instantly and involuntarily become conscious that he was present at some great

53

world-renowned action."[6] The foreground figures of Edmund Pendleton and Richard Henry Lee provide a study in contrast: the agitated Pendleton lunges in protest, while the seated Lee clenches his chair and nearby table as he ponders the ramifications of Henry's speech.

Rothermel's success in visualizing this historic event was extolled by the *North American and United States Gazette*:

> No one who looks upon the picture can fail to be struck with the graphic force of fancy and execution with which the reality has been copied. The lofty, inspired attitude of the orator—the rapt countenance of Lee, whose gaze seems comprehensive of the august revolutionary drama that impended—the anxious, deprecating manner of Pendleton—the rage, the terror, the interest, and every emotional expression...have been caught by the painter with rare power, and transferred in living colors to his canvas.[7]

Compositionally, *Patrick Henry*, like many other grand academic pictures, suggests a host of pictorial associations, affinities, and possible sources. These include the antique *Augustus of Prima Porta*; Peter Paul Rubens's 1627–28 *Mystical Marriage of St. Catherine*; Caroline Watson's 1782 print after Robert Edge Pine, *Garrick Reciting an Ode to Shakespeare* (fig. 9); John Sartain's undated engraving after George Henry Harlow's *The Trial of Queen Catherine*;

Fig. 10   Godefroid Guffens. *Rouget de Lisle Singing "The Marseillaise,"* 1849, oil on canvas, 52 × 67 in. Museum of American Art of the Pennsylvania Academy of the Fine Arts, Philadelphia; Academy purchase

Fig. 11 Robert Whitechurch after Peter Frederick Rothermel, *The United States Senate A.D. 1850*, 1855, engraving, 27 × 34 3/16 in. National Portrait Gallery, Smithsonian Institution; gift of Mrs. Richard K. Doud

Washington Allston's 1817–43 *Belshazzar's Feast*; George Cooke's ca. 1834 *Patrick Henry Arguing the Parson's Cause at Hanover Court House*; an illustration of Henry's speech in Benson Lossing's 1847 *Seventeen Hundred and Seventy-Six*; Belgian painter Godefroid Guffens's 1849 *Rouget de Lisle Singing the "Marseillaise"* (fig. 10); and Rothermel's own 1850 *Murray's Defence of Toleration* (see fig. 3).[8] The Lossing and the Guffens (which Rothermel probably saw at the 1850 annual exhibition of the Pennsylvania Academy) may have influenced two of his preliminary compositional drawings (see cat. 8a). In turn, *Patrick Henry* affected a number of later Rothermel compositions, including *United States Senate, A.D. 1850* (fig. 11).

Each subscriber to the Art Union for 1852 received Alfred Jones's engraving after the painting (see cat. 8b). Before the distribution of Art Union prizes, the painting was exhibited at the Mercantile Library Association in Baltimore, the Rotunda of the United States Capitol in Washington, and at the Richmond, Virginia, library.[9] It was in Richmond that one journal paused after praising the painting for its subject and form: "We are sorry, however, to say that one cannot recommend it very highly for its historic truth. In fact, it rather contradicts all our established ideas of the scene and speech which it aims to illustrate."[10] Indeed, contrary to the numerous claims that the painting faithfully transcribed the incident, Rothermel's composition presents the past according to the artist's interpretations and interests. Rothermel's Patrick Henry is a man of aristocratic elan, not Wirt's yeoman whose "dress and manners were still those of the plain planter."[11] Furthermore, Rothermel's setting has architectural grandeur and women spectators. Yet, despite (or because of) these historical inaccuracies, the composition succeeds in offering a dramatic and inspiring image of American history.

Like Emanuel Leutze's contemporary painting, *Washington Crossing the Delaware*, Rothermel's *Patrick Henry* is an idealized composition filled with details that aim to elevate the hero, to inculcate patriotism, and to please the eye. Both paintings, to paraphrase Pablo Picasso, are lies that lead to the truth.

The "truth" that concerned Rothermel is the ideal of American resolve to take a stand. The figure of Patrick Henry embodies this belief; "the whole expression [of Henry] is that of a powerful mind and resolute will...[one that] carries the beholder back to the times when our countrymen were equal in energy and perserverance to any emergency." This was also a criticism of the present—a period experiencing a tearing of the social and political fabric, as sectionalist interests pulled in opposite directions. Patrick Henry's daring "to throw the gauntlet in the face of tyranny and oppression," offered a model of virtuous action.[12]

Yet the thrown glove, if not a gauntlet, lying on the floor is an intriguing detail: why is it there? whose is it? how did it get there? Presumably it belongs to Henry, but, where is his other glove? The one figure who wears a glove is the British officer drawing his sword. If it is his, has he thrown it down—from quite a distance, given the sharply receding space—to challenge Henry? More likely, it appears to be Henry's metaphoric gauntlet made literal. Placed on the same vertical sight line as his emphatically raised hand, the glove suggests a physical violence (it having been flung down) that parallels the emotional violence of Henry's passionate rhetoric.

On December 31, 1852, the annual distribution of the Philadelphia Art Union took place: *Patrick Henry* went to G. W. Grier of Philadelphia. By 1865 the painting belonged to Joseph Harrison and was prominently featured in what many considered the finest private art gallery in the country.[13]

[1] "Rothermel's New National Painting," *Sun* (Philadelphia), February 16, 1852, p. 2. This article, appearing on a Monday, indicates that the painting was placed in the Art Union gallery on Saturday.

[2] "The Philadelphia Art-Union," *Graham's Magazine* 40 (March 1852): 326. Earlier Joseph Sill had written about the then unfinished painting: "[it] bears more than common marks of skill & genius, and which will undoubtedly be improved as it advances. I think it will increase his fame, & add to his fortune too—I hope" (October 10, 1851, Joseph Sill Diary, 9:443, HSP).

[3] "A New Feature in Our Plan," *Philadelphia Art Union Reporter* 1 (March and April 1851): 39. Rothermel received $1000 for the painting.

[4] Rothermel chaired a group of 35 artists and 7 amateurs who "by way of showing our appreciation" to the Art Union, "do hereby pledge ourselves individually, to present to the Art Union of Philadelphia, an original work of art, of a value not less than fifty dollars" (*Philadelphia Art Union Reporter* 1 (January 1852): 146). Their action was in response

to the inability of the Art Union to make its annual distribution prizes for 1851.

[5] William Wirt, *Sketches of the Life and Character of Patrick Henry* (6th rev. ed.; New York: McElrath, Bangs, 1833), p. 83. The book appeared in 1817 and went through many editions.

[6] "The Philadelphia Art-Union," p. 326. To help identify the major figures in the composition, the Art Union published a key to the painting on June 1, 1852.

[7] Before the picture was completed, one writer observed: "The greatness of this scene appeals to the mind rather than to the eye, and we doubt whether Mr. Rothermel with all his ability, will be able to make it as striking and impressive as Mr. Wirt has done by his simple narration. We have been told, however, that the work, so far as it has progressed, is very satisfactory, and we shall be well pleased to find that we are false prophets" ("New Work by Rothermel," *Bulletin of the American Art-Union* 4 [July 1851]: 64).

[8] John W. McCoubrey pointed out the affinity to the Rubens long ago. One contemporary journalist linked the Guffens and Rothermel paintings, but to the detriment of each: "The whole scene [of *Patrick Henry*] is ridiculous.... The great American orator looks as if he was leading off in a Jacobin club; his up-turned eye—and his whole attitude—is a most farcical attempt to portray inspiration. The thing is a fit companion to the De Lisle of Guffens" ("Fine Arts: Washington Exhibition," *Albion*, March 26, 1853, p. 153. Elsewhere in the same issue, the Guffens picture is termed ridiculous.

[9] In announcing that the painting would travel to Baltimore, the Philadelphia *Sun* noted: "The attention which it [the painting] elicited at first has not decreased, but the gallery is crowded, at all hours, by the taste and fashion of the day" ("Rothermel's Patrick Henry," *Sun* [March 22, 1852], p. 1). Announcement of the painting's exhibition in Baltimore is found in the Baltimore *Sun*, April 1, 1852, p. 3. The painting was there through April 20. Another Baltimore newspaper called a painting of "great merit" (*American and Commercial Daily Advertiser* April 2, 1852, p. 2.). "Rothermel's Picture of Patrick Henry," *Virginia Historical Register* 5 (October 1852): 236, states that the painting has been on view and that many people have seen it.

[10] "Rothermel's Picture of Patrick Henry," p. 236.

[11] Wirt, *Patrick Henry*, pp. 52, 62. Rothermel realized the changes he was making: "Text does not justify putting upon him a cloak—nor full dress nor such as Lawyers have even[?]—nor Statesmen in Legislative assemblies [?] etc" (manuscript presumed to be in Rothermel's hand, Red Hill, Patrick Henry National Memorial Foundation).

[12] "Rothermel's New National Painting," p. 1. For a fascinating interpretation of the painting as an image of millenial thought, see Gail Husch, " 'Something Coming': Prophecy and American Painting, 1848–1854," Ph.D. diss., University of Delaware, 1992, 1:313–22. For a discussion of the painting and Joseph Harrison, Jr., see Carolyn Sue Himelick Nutty, "Joseph Harrison, Jr. (1810–1874): Philadelphia Art Collector," Ph.D. diss., University of Delaware, 1993, 1:349–53.

[13] "Drawing of the Philadelphia Art Union," *Sun* (Philadelphia), January 1, 1853, p. 5; Harrison lent the work to the Northwestern Sanitary Fair, Chicago, in 1865.

Study for Patrick Henry in the House of Burgesses in Virginia, Delivering His Celebrated Speech against the Stamp Act

Cat. 8a
Study for *Patrick Henry in the House of Burgesses in Virginia, Delivering His Celebrated Speech against the Stamp Act*
1851
Graphite and wash on paper,
16 × 12½ inches
(40.6 × 31.8 cm)
The Patrick Henry Memorial Foundation, Brookneal, Virginia

This vertical drawing is undoubtedly the last of three surviving compositional studies for the large painting. The earliest (fig. 12) shows Patrick Henry raising both his arms. The next (fig. 13), depicting Henry pointing one arm, is nearer in conception to the final image. In both earlier drawings the horizontal format and centralized hero, indicate the likely influence of Godefroid Guffens's *Rouget de Lisle Singing the "Marseillaise."* By then switching to the vertical format and a strong diagonal axis, Rothermel focused and strengthened the composition. That the third drawing is squared off, suggests it served as the final drawing that was transferred to the canvas. Although the drawing is extremely close to the painting, it includes fewer figures, Henry has a less dynamic gesture, and no glove lies in the foreground.

Fig. 12 Study for *Patrick Henry in the House of Burgesses of Virginia, Delivering His Celebrated Speech against the Stamp Act*, 1851, ink, wash and graphite on paper, 6 × 9 in. Courtesy of The Patrick Henry Memorial Foundation, Brookneal, Virginia

Fig. 13 Study for *Patrick Henry in the House of Burgesses of Virginia, Delivering His Celebrated Speech against the Stamp Act*, 1851, pencil on paper, 8⅞ × 11¾ in. Gil E. Pablo, M.D. Collection

Patrick Henry in the House of Burgesses of Virginia, Delivering His Celebrated Speech against the Stamp Act

Cat. 8b
Patrick Henry in the House of Burgesses of Virginia, Delivering His Celebrated Speech against the Stamp Act
Alfred Jones after Peter F. Rothermel
1852–1853
Engraving, 32 × 18 inches
(81.3 × 45.7 cm)
The Library Company of Philadelphia

Every member of the Art Union of Philadelphia for 1852 who paid the $5 subscription fee received this print. One reporter touted the engraving would be "worthy of a place in the most elegant parlor," and a journal announced that "the picture itself, and the engraving of it, will form an era in the history of American art, as the subject itself did in the history of American independence."[1] The print was slow getting to members, as Jones had not finished it by the end of 1852. Nevertheless, the engraving did become widely known and collected. Rembrandt Peale kept a print in his studio.[2] Throughout the twentieth century it was used as an illustration in numerous history books and advertisements. Yet the engraving also provides an index to the declining interest in grand historical images. When the Art Union of Philadelphia began operating again in 1882 after a hiatus of nearly 30 years, Jones's engraving was one of seventeen prints offered to members: 2 people out of 90 chose it; in 1883, 2 out of 134 selected it; and in 1885/86, 3 out of 500.[3]

---

[1] "Rothermel's Picture," Philadelphia *Sunday Dispatch* March 7, 1852, p. 2; "The Philadelphia Art-Union," *Graham's Magazine* 40 (March 1852): 326.

[2] John A. Mahey, "The Studio of Rembrandt Peale," *American Art Journal* 1 (Fall 1969): 28.

[3] *Annual Report of the Board of Managers of the Art Union of Philadelphia, for the Promotion of the Arts of Design in the United States* for the years 1882, 1883, 1885/86. A clipping from the Philadelphia *Inquirer*, August 17, 1895 (Scrapbooks of Thomas Hovenden, Archives of American Art, Smithsonian Institution) indicates this was a dramatic change from the previous decades when the print "hung in so many many households that it is doubtful if any other American artist was so widely known."

The Banishment of Roger Williams

Cat. 9
The Banishment of Roger Williams
ca. 1851–1852
Inscribed lower right:
   P. F. Rothermel
Oil on canvas,
35 1/2 × 28 1/2 inches
(90.2 × 72.4 cm)
Rhode Island Historical Society

In this dramatic composition, Rothermel placed the hero in a frozen and threatening wilderness. Roger Williams, framed by large trees whose branches and roots menacingly reach towards him, pauses with eyes turned heavenward as a blast of frigid air blows his coat and cape back. In one hand his walking stick bends to his determination and perseverance; in the other hand he holds a Bible, his finger marking a passage. By this depiction of Williams literally touching the word of God, Rothermel emphasized the banished religious leader's source of strength and inspiration.

Rothermel's highly romantic and fictive image (no likeness of Roger Williams exists) coheres to Williams's account of his bitter winter journey "exposed to the mercy of an howling Wilderness in Frost and Snow, &c."[1] Williams had fled Salem—seen in the lower left distance "bathed in the orange and red of sunset, or, perchance, a hellish glow"—in January 1636, following an October 1635 sentence of banishment for holding opinions "erroneous and very dangerous."[2] (These included his notion that the American Indians, not the colonists, were the true owners of the land). He wandered in the wilderness for fourteen weeks before settling at Narragansett Bay and helping to found Providence and the Rhode Island colony.

The striking, aggressive stance Rothermel gave the hero resonates with figures as divergent as the Hellenistic *Borghese Warrior* and George Washington in Emanuel Leutze's *Washington Crossing the Delaware* (1851).[3] In its heroic realism, the composition shows an affinity to the sublimity of Jacques-Louis David's *Napoleon Crossing the Alps* (1800) and the directness of Paul Delaroche's later (1848) version of the same subject. Rothermel also may have been familiar with an illustration of Williams in John Frost's 1846 *Book of the Colonies*.[4] While the painting differs from book illustration in showing a standing Williams, both include similar walking sticks, high crowned hats, and bleak wintry landscapes.

The artist likely executed *The Banishment of Roger Williams* in 1851 or 1852, and it was among the prizes distributed by the Philadelphia Art Union in 1853.[5]

---

[1] Williams as quoted in Edwin S. Gaustad, *Liberty of Conscience: Roger Williams in America* (Grand Rapids, Mich.: William B. Eerdmans Publishing Co., 1991), p. 46.

[2] Bradford F. Swan, "Roger Williams Painting Viewed," *Providence Sunday Journal*, December 5, 1943, p. 22; Henry Chupack, *Roger Williams* (New York: Twayne Publishers, 1969), p. 47.

[3] For a connection to another Hellenistic work, the *Gaulish Chieftain Killing Himself*, see *The Classical Spirit in American Portraiture* (Providence: Bell Gallery, Brown University, 1976), p. 92.

[4] John Frost, *The Book of the Colonies* (New York: D. Appleton; Philadelphia: G. S. Appleton, 1846), p. 178. Intriguingly, Frost's illustration of de Soto discovering the Mississippi (p. 57) is a rearrangement of figures in Rothermel's 1843 painting of the same subject. The writer and painter probably knew each other, for Frost owned two Rothermel paintings that were exhibited at the Artists' Fund Society: *Death of Old Morality* in 1841, and *The Hawking Party: A Scene from the "Betrothed"* in 1842.

[5] "The Art Union Distribution of Prizes," *Public Ledger*, January 1, 1853, p. 1. The work went to a Mrs. Paul.

David Playing the Harp before Saul

Cat. 10
David Playing the Harp before Saul
1852–1853
Inscribed lower right:
  P.F. Rothermel
Oil on canvas, 44 × 52 inches
(111.8 × 132.1 cm)
Philadelphia Museum of Art:
gift of Florence Foerderer Tonner
in memory of her parents,
Robert H. Foerderer and
Caroline Fisher Foerderer to the
Lutheran Church in America

According to I Samuel 16:14–23,

Now the Spirit of the LORD departed from Saul, and an evil spirit from the LORD tormented him. And Saul's servants said to him, "Behold now, an evil spirit from God is tormenting you. Let our lord now command your servants, who are before you, to seek out a man who is skilful in playing the lyre; and when the evil spirit from God is upon you, he will play it, and you will be well." So Saul said to his servants, "Provide for me a man who can play well, and bring him to me."…And David came to Saul, and entered his service. And Saul loved him greatly, and he became his armor-bearer.…And whenever the evil spirit from God was upon Saul, David took the lyre and played it with his hand; so Saul was refreshed, and was well, and the evil spirit departed from him.

Rothermel gave David a harp rather than lyre and rendered the moment when the young man begins to play for the downcast, possessed king, as the royal retinue stands by anxiously. Like so many of Rothermel's compositions this one focuses on a scene of confrontation; however, here the two protagonists confront not each other, but the evil spirit.

When Joseph Sill saw the unfinished painting in Rothermel's studio on November 20, 1852, he noted that it was intended for Mr. C. Jones.[1] The Pennsylvania Academy's 1854 annual exhibition catalogue further identified Jones as Caleb Jones, a Philadelphia merchant.

Related to the painting is a drawing (fig. 14) that lays out the general composition but lacks the background papyrus column and the mother and child in the lower left. Another drawing shows a later episode—David observing the sleeping Saul (see cat. 56).

[1] November 20, 1852, Joseph Sill Diary, 10:176, HSP.

Fig. 14 [cat. 55] *David Playing before Saul*, 1852.
Gil E. Pablo, M.D. Collection

Milton and His Daughters

Cat. 11
Milton and His Daughters
1853
Oil on canvas, 43 × 53 inches
(109.2 × 134.6 cm)
Harry Ransom Humanities
Research Center, The University
of Texas at Austin

On seeing this painting in Rothermel's studio in 1852, Joseph Sill decided that it promised to be a good picture.[1] Sill did not mention if the work had been commissioned, but it appeared in the 1853 Pennsylvania Academy of the Fine Arts annual exhibition as belonging to C. Cope. Undoubtedly, this was Caleb Cope, a successful merchant who went on to serve as president of the academy from 1859 to 1871. The exhibition catalogue entry for the painting included lines from book 3 of *Paradise Lost*:

> Seasons return, but not to me return
> Day, or the sweet approach of eve or morn;
> Or sight of vernal bloom, or summer rose;
> Or flocks, or herd, or human face divine;
> But clouds instead, and ever-during dark
> Surrounds me.[2]

The eminence of John Milton, the seventeenth-century English poet and political writer, remained high in Rothermel's day, and his work and life offered European and American painters abundant subjects.[3] Rothermel's composition depicts the blind Milton dictating his epic poem *Paradise Lost* (1667) to his daughters. While a number of engraved portraits of Milton were

Fig. 15 [cat. 67] *Study of a Head of a Man in Historical Costume*, ca. 1857.
Gil E. Pablo, M.D. Collection

available to the artist, he apparently drew his likenesss from a 1794 print he owned.[4] This engraving, after an image by George Vertue, portrays Milton at age sixty-two; Milton would have been about fifty-nine at the time of Rothermel's scene. Rothermel's portrayal of Milton influenced his later oil study of a younger, unidentified man (fig. 15).

Milton and His Daughters includes a shadowy portrait hanging above the poet, a chamber organ, and books scattered about the floor in typical Rothermel fashion.[5] Writing absorbs two of the girls, while the third listens intently to her father's words. As a group they suggest a literary "Three Graces," and exemplify filial devotion. In reality, the Milton brood was far from happy, and the girls did not serve gladly. As a later biographer put it:

> They found it irksome....One knows not how many pictures and engravings there have been by artists, or many more there will be, representing the blind Milton seated in state, dictating *Paradise Lost* to one or other of this three daughters, all reverently grouped around him, or kneeling beside him, with looks of affection and admiration. The sad

fact is otherwise....[T]hey were, all three, in dumb rebellion.[6]

Rothermel, himself a father of three, chose to perpetuate the mythic and reassuring scene of domestic tranquility and familial dedication. This theme also occurs in two of his compositional drawings—*Reading the Bible* (collection of Gil E. Pablo, M.D.) and *The Grandfather* (fig. 16)—that do not directly relate to *Milton and His Daughters* as studies but do share some characteristics. Like the painting, they show an older man seated with young women. The placement of the older man and woman in each drawing is similar to that in the painting. Although not dated, their style suggests they were executed about the same time as the *Milton*.

At least one nineteenth-century writer pointed to a link between the writer and artist:

> The department of art to which Mr. Rothermel has devoted his life requires the highest class of talent, as each picture is a tragedy and epic combined for the scene—at the visual part of it—must be purely the ideal conception of the author. In this respect his work is exactly like those of Milton and Dante in describing the wonders of heaven and hell, which they had never seen.[7]

[1] June 10, 1852, Joseph Sill Diary, 10:82, HSP. Sill refers to the work as "Milton Dictating Paradise Lost to his 2 Daughters." On November 20, 1852, Sill (Diary, 10:176) decided that he preferred the Milton to *David before Saul* on which Rothermel was working.

[2] *Catalogue of the Thirtieth Annual Exhibition of the Pennsylvania Academy of the Fine Arts* (Philadelphia, 1853), p. 8.

[3] See John T. Shawcross, *John Milton and Influence* (Pittsburgh: Duquesne University Press, 1991), pp. 139–55; Marcia R. Pointon, *Milton and English Art* (Toronto: University of Toronto Press, 1970). Among artists Rothermel admired, Thomas Sully painted *Milton and His Daughter* (1816) and Eugene Delacroix rendered *Milton Dictating to His Daughters* (Salon of 1827).

[4] This print is part of a privately owned collection of Rothermel materials.

[5] Emanuel Leutze's *Cromwell and Milton* (1854) shows Milton playing the organ.

[6] David Masson, *The Life of John Milton* (1880; reprint, New York: Peter Smith, 1946), 6:448.

[7] M[oses] Auge, *Lives of the Eminent Dead and Biographical Notices of Prominent Living Citizens of Montgomery County, Pa.* (Norristown: M. Auge, 1879), p. 427.

Thou Art the Man

Cat. 12
Thou Art the Man
Inscribed lower left:
  P. F. Rothermel / 1854
Oil on canvas,
50 × 62¼ inches
(127 × 158.1 cm)
Museum of American Art of the
Pennsylvania Academy of the
Fine Arts, Philadelphia; gift of
Craig Heberton[1]

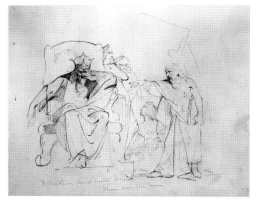

Fig. 17 [cat. 58] Study for *Thou Art the Man*,
ca. 1853. Gil E. Pablo, M.D. Collection

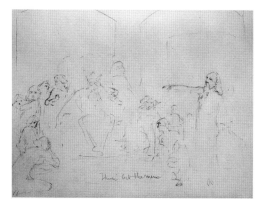

Fig. 18 [cat. 59] Study for *Thou Art the Man*,
ca. 1853. Gil E. Pablo, M.D. Collection

One of Rothermel's most beautifully painted works, *Thou Art the Man* exhibits the artist's penchant for conveying dramatic tension by pitting a standing accusatory figure against a seated figure of debased authority. In it Rothermel rendered the Old Testament account of the confrontation between King David and Nathan the Prophet. The king, having taken Bathsheba, the wife of Uriah the Hittite, has sent her husband into the forefront of battle to be killed. Nathan rebukes David by relating a parable of a rich man who steals the only lamb of a poor man:

> And David's anger was greatly kindled against the man; and he said to Nathan, "As the LORD liveth, the man that hath done this *thing* shall surely die: And he shall restore the lamb fourfold, because he did this thing, and because he had no pity." And Nathan said to David, "Thou *art* the man....Wherefore hast thou despised the commandment of the LORD, to do evil in his sight?" [II Samuel 12:5–9.]

Rothermel conveyed the weight of the declaration by the prophet's powerful body language and by the way the magnificently garbed king recoils. The composition not only resembles the artist's *Patrick Henry*, but also surviving sketchbook pages show a *Patrick Henry* study adjacent to a drawing for *Thou Art the Man* (fig. 17). This preliminary compositional drawing and another (see fig. 18) show David lowering his head in shame; however, the painting presents a more forceful reaction. The painting also has a more dramatic distance between the two protagonists and in it there are many figures that are only suggested in the sketchier of the two drawings. To reinforce the darkness of the king's deed, the artist painted Nathan's shadow threateningly creeping up the steps, and the shadow of his crook ominously suggesting a scythe. As in a number of Rothermel compositions, the crowd of figures offers a variety of emotional responses to the highly charged moment.[2] Rothermel created a composition that impresses itself immediately upon the viewer through its dramatic scene, exotic setting, and rich color, yet it sustains viewer enjoyment by the provocative portrayal of each figure's reaction to the event.

[1] The painting has for many years carried the date of "1884." Stylistically speaking, such a late date seemed questionable; the work also appeared too ambitious in scale and composition for the artist's declining abilities in the 1880s. Arguing for an earlier date are two compositional drawings from the early 1850s, and Joseph Sill's 1854 diary entries that record Rothermel at work on *David, Nathan, and the Prophet* and nearly completed with it (February 17 and June 10, 1854, Joseph Sill Diary, 10: 441, 509, HSP). Under a microscope the date appears to read "1854". My thanks to Elyssa B. Kane of the Pennsylvania Academy of the Fine Arts for her assistance in this matter.

[2] Even more than his *Patrick Henry*, this composition suggests familiarity with Washington Allston's *Belshazzar's Feast* (1817–43). Indeed, like many Rothermel works, *Thou Art the Man* seems to synthesize and resonate with other artists' works. For instance, the setting recalls compositions by English painter John Martin, and the seated scribe at the left suggests the influence of Michelangelo. The drawings, and much less so the painting, imply an awareness of the Valentine Green mezzotint of Benjamin West's *Nathan and David* (ca. 1775).

Unidentified Woman

Cat. 13
Unidentified Woman
Undated
Oil on canvas,
30 3/16 × 25 inches
(76.7 × 63.5 cm)
Museum of American Art of the
Pennsylvania Academy of the
Fine Arts, Philadelphia; bequest
of Josephine A. Natt

In this portrait, Rothermel focused attention on a fashionably dressed sitter by having her fill the composition, by setting her off against the vaguest of backgrounds, and by placing an intriguing element (a lamp or architectural detail?) at left. Especially impressive in this painting is Rothermel's fluid brushwork in the sleeves and the fabric across the bottom of the composition. His apparent ease in handling the paint and skill in creating a convincing sense of this woman's presence suggest that the work dates from the mid 1850s to mid 1860s. The portrait conveys an appealing freshness and immediacy, while evidencing the artist's competence in emulating the romantic elegance of Thomas Sully's work. As such, it represents the survival of English high art traditions in Philadelphia, where artists, like Rothermel, "kept hallowed the memories of the grand style."[1]

[1] Harrison S. Morris, "Philadelphia's Contribution to American Art," *Century Magazine* 69 (March 1905): 723. Morris was then the managing director of the Pennsylvania Academy of the Fine Arts.

Edwin Forrest as King Lear

Cat. 14
Edwin Forrest as King Lear
1856
Oil on canvas, 30 × 25 inches
(76.2 × 63.5 cm)
The Actors' Fund of America,
currently displayed in the
Edwin Forrest wing of The
Actors' Fund Nursing Home,
Englewood, New Jersey

Edwin Forrest, a Philadelphian by birth, loomed large in nineteenth-century American theater. He was the first native-born actor to become a star. He knew Rothermel and even commissioned a work of art to help pay for the artist's study abroad: he asked Rothermel to copy a portrait of the great French actor, François Joseph Talma.[1]

Rothermel's striking portrait of Forrest in the guise of one of his best known stage persona is directly related to his 1858 grand painting, *King Lear* (cat. 15). The turn of the head, the rendering of hair and beard, and the intense expression are virtually identical both—only the crown differs. This portrait provided the visage of the king in that full-length painting.

The literature on Rothermel claims that Forrest posed for the artist in London in 1856, perhaps because Rothermel himself said that he made a study for *King Lear* while there: "[I] took the study from the pose of Forrest, but it is not like Forrest. He was of such a peculiar style that the more Forrest the less *Lear* I got into the painting."[2] This portrait—which may or may not be the "study" Rothermel mentions—indeed shows sharper and longer facial features than are evident in other images of Forrest. And a problem exists with the idea of Forrest posing for Rothermel in London: it is highly unlikely that Forrest was in England at the time. Having received an unfavorable ruling in an alimony case in July 1856, the actor curtailed his autumn performance schedule with an eye to retiring to his new house in Philadelphia.[3] No record of his traveling abroad at this time exists, and no mention of the artist's meeting him in London appears in Rothermel's notebook. Rothermel's comment that he "took the study from the pose of Forrest," does not necessarily mean that the actor actually posed for him. It could indicate that the artist worked from a memory of having witnessed Forrest perform as Lear, or that he worked from a photograph. The latter is most likely.

An account book of Philadelphia photographer Frederick Debourg Richards shows that Rothermel purchased a three-quarter size portrait of Forrest on July 9, 1856.[4] Secured a month before the artist left on his European sojourn (with the commission for the large painting of King Lear for Joseph Harrison, Jr., already set), this photograph probably provided "the pose of Forrest" for his study in London. Whether or not this portrait of Forrest is what Rothermel termed a "study," the portrait does depict the head of Lear seen in the final painting.

An entry for April 7, 1858, in the artist's notebook indicates that he had just sold the "Original head of Lear—also sketch of Lear" to James Vansyckle.[5] The dispersal of these suggests that the large painting commissioned by Harrison, was completed, or nearly so.

---

[1] May 19, 1856, Rothermel notebook. Rothermel was to receive $200 for the painting.

[2] "A Venerable Artist," *Public Ledger* March 19, 1890, p.3.

[3] Richard Moody, *Edwin Forrest: First Star of the American Stage* (New York: Alfred A. Knopf, 1960), pp. 330–34.

[4] The account book entry is dated July 9, 1856. I am grateful to Christine Schultz of Schwarz Gallery, Philadelphia for bringing the Rothermel page from Richards's book to my attention.

[5] April 7, 1858, Rothermel notebook.

King Lear

Cat. 15
King Lear
Inscribed lower right:
  P. F. Rothermel / Rome 1858
Oil on canvas,
125 ½ × 87 ¼ inches
(318.8 × 221.6 cm)
Schwarz Gallery, Philadelphia

This immense work depicting act 4 scene 6 of Shakespeare's play was painted in Rome for Joseph Harrison, Jr., of Philadelphia. The *Crayon*, noted in its November 1858 issue:

> Rothermel's "King Lear," lately arrived from Rome, forms one of the attractions of Mr. Harrison's gallery. The scene chosen by the artist is that where the raving Lear is reminded of his true condition by a question of the blind Gloster, who is led by Edgar.
>
> *Gloster.* The trick of that voice I do well remember: Is't not the king?
> *Lear.* Ay, every inch a king.
>
> This picture is thus far Mr. Rothermel's best work.[1]

A most impressive painting, the composition relies on powerful contrasts of light and dark and striking rendering of figures—especially that of the majestically deranged Lear—to express the tragic and the sublime. Lear's weedy lightning-bolt scepter and crown, which confirm the king's irrationality and agitated mental state, follow Cordelia's description of her father. The particular subject perfectly matched Rothermel's propensity for the dramatic, the expressive, and the colorful.

Among the commissions listed in Rothermel's European notebook appears the entry "Jos. Harrison—Forrest as Lear—Every Inch a King," with a price of $3,000. "Forrest" is Edwin Forrest, noted Shakespearean actor, Philadelphian, and Rothermel patron, who, according to tradition, posed for the painter (see cat. 14). Of all of the actor's roles, Lear was considered Forrest's greatest, and most people believed they had never seen a better portrayal.[2] The actor agreed. Indeed, once when complimented on how well he played Lear, Forrest exclaimed: "*Play Lear!* what do you mean, sir? I do not *play Lear!*...By God, sir! I *am Lear!*[3] This painting represents a wonderful coming together of two artists given to grandiloquent statements: As one correspondent put it: "It may be [Rothermel's] calling to paint grand scenes, just as Mr. Forrest thinks it is his to do high tragedy."[4]

King Lear hung as a featured object in Harrison's Rittenhouse Square mansion, the art gallery in which was esteemed to hold the finest private collection in Philadelphia. Also in the gallery was another *King Lear*, of similar size and composition, by Belgian artist J. B. Wittkamp.[5] In comparing the two paintings, an 1876 writer asserted that "Rothermel's is infinitely the best" and that "evidence of perfect knowledge of the powers of color is ample."[6]

Rothermel's painting was exhibited under various titles: *King Lear in His Madness* (Washington Art Association, 1859), *King Lear* (Rhode Island Society for Domestic Industry, 1867), and *King Lear, Gloster, and Edgar* (Harrison Collection catalogue, 1870). The work appears in Jeremy Wilson's

1858 painting, *Rothermel in his Roman Studio* (fig. 7). Rothermel also executed a small version (1859) of the composition and two other related pictures treating the theme of Lear and Cordelia (cats. 44 and 61).[7]

[1] "Philadelphia," *Crayon* 5 (November 1858): 329.

[2] Richard Moody, *Edwin Forrest: First Star of the American Stage* (New York: Alfred A. Knopf, 1960), p. 404. A reproduction (William Winter, *Shakespeare on Stage* [2d ser.; New York: Moffat, Yard, 1915], facing p. 438), also shows Forrest as Lear in act 4 scene 6. Although Forrest wears a more elaborate, imperial costume than in Rothermel's painting and holds the sheaf of weeds in his left hand, the print shows striking similarities to the painting in the actor's general pose and facial expression.

[3] Lawrence Barrett, *Edwin Forrest* (Boston: James R. Osgood, 1881), p. 157.

[4] L., "Art—Philadelphia Art Notes," *Round Table* (New York), April 9, 1864, p. 266.

[5] The Wittkamp painting is unlocated; a reproduction appears in *Paintings, Statuary, etc., the Remainder of the Collection of the Late Joseph Harrison, Jr. and Belonging to the Estate of Mrs. Sarah Harrison Deceased* (Philadelphia: Philadelphia Art Galleries, 1912), no. 27.

[6] John Colonna, "Art in Philadelphia," clipping from Philadelphia *Inquirer*, November 1876, "Newspaper Clippings" book, pp. 62–64, Papers of James Lawrence Claghorn, Archives of American Art, Smithsonian Institution.

[7] The small version measures 31 × 23 1/2 inches. Formerly owned by Anthony C. Schmidt Fine Arts, it is now in a private collection.

Christic and the Doctors

Cat. 16
Christ and the Doctors
Inscribed lower right:
  P. F. Rothermel 1861
Oil on canvas,
62 $^{1}/_{4}$ × 75 inches
(158.1 × 190.5 cm)
The Reading Public Museum,
Reading, Pennsylvania

This tightly packed composition clearly relates to the artist's *Patrick Henry* of ten years earlier (see cat. 8). The Christ child—who strikes a pose only slightly different from that of the Virginia legislator—occupies the picture's center and is being ringed by the massive half-figures of the doctors, several of whom exhibit intense facial expressions reminiscent of those in the *Patrick Henry*. As in that earlier work, the hero has dramatically spoken words that inspire, intrigue, and antagonize his audience.

Rothermel took his theme from Luke 2:41–51, which describes how the twelve year old sat in the temple in Jerusalem among the teachers (doctors) "listening to them and asking them questions; and all who heard him were amazed at his understanding and his answers." As was his wont, Rothermel enlarged upon the dramatic moment by rendering a dynamically positioned Christ surrounded by exotically turbanned figures and monumental architecture.

A large decorative column frames Christ's head, compositionally focusing attention on the child, while symbolically asserting him as a pillar of strength and truth. This column and another on the left show figural relief sculpture, stylized acanthus decorations, and a twisting shaft. (This last motif suggests the spiraling columns of the Temple of Jerusalem and their baroque manifestation in Bernini's baldacchino, both in Saint Peter's, a site Rothermel surely visited during his two-year stay in Rome.) Rothermel charged the space between these two columns with Christ's upward thrusting arm and the intensely concentrated gaze of one of the doctors. In the distance stands a Doric temple. The juxtaposition of Christ's hand and this temple suggests the authority of the Word over paganism.

Rothermel completed the painting around mid November 1861, for on the 25th he wrote Ferdinand Dreer: "I would be pleased to show my Picture of Christ & the Doctors on view at my studio until Friday next."[1] Six months later a pleased Rothermel wrote to fellow artist Russell Smith: "Your very kind note is before me, your favorable opinion of the little picture of Christ & the Doctors is exceedingly gratifying to me."[2] The painting also garnered praise when it appeared in the annual exhibition of the Pennsylvania Academy: "The new historical pictures which will draw attention [include] "Christ among the Doctors," by Rothermel, in his characteristic style, that usually brings out the meaning of the picture by the variety of personages introduced, each actor strongly marked in his countenance or costume."[3]

The academy exhibition catalogue listed the work as *Christ and the Doctors* and as owned by Mrs. Vansyckle, presumably the wife of James Vansyckle, an important patron. Two years later at the the art exhibition of the Great Central Fair in Philadelphia it was labeled *Christ in the Temple*.

[1] Rothermel to Ferdinand Dreer, November 25, 1861, Dreer Collection, HSP. Rothermel to Robert C. Davis, November 26, 1861 (Charles Roberts Autographs of American Artists Collection, Haverford College Library), is a nearly identical letter.

[2] Rothermel to Russell Smith, May 26, 1862, Smith Family Papers, Archives of American Art, Smithsonian Institution.

[3] "The Fine Arts in Philadelphia," *Godey's Lady's Book* 65 (August 1862): 196–97. Rothermel's work was only one of two history paintings singled out in the review, the other being Christian Schuessele's *Zeisberger Preaching to the Indians*. Rothermel's painting received negative criticism in 1864: a reviewer thought the painting did not enhance the artist's reputation and suggested that a better title for it would be "The Deck of the Great Eastern in a Storm" (L., "Art—Philadelphia Art Notes," *Round Table*, June 25, 1864, p. 27).

First Reading of the Declaration of Independence

Cat. 17
First Reading of the Declaration of Independence
1861
Oil on canvas,
41 $\frac{1}{2}$ × 67 $\frac{1}{2}$ inches
(105.4 × 171.5 cm)
Union League of Philadelphia

The intense dramatic focus characteristic of Rothermel's history paintings gives way in *First Reading of the Declaration of Independence* to a more episodic composition. Various figures in the randomly dispersed crowd compete for our attention with the historic reading in the distance. By a seemingly natural arrangement, Rothermel imbues the work with realism, a quality also evident in his *State House, the Day of the Battle of Germantown* (cat. 19) and *The Battle of Gettysburg: Pickett's Charge* (cat. 26). Yet, Rothermel's realism is tempered by his academic commitment to treating figures as characters who strike poses and play roles. His figures, enlivened by intense reds and whites, act out the story, which is always key for Rothermel.

First Reading of the Declaration of Independence shows the public proclamation of that revolutionary document in Philadelphia on July 8, 1776. The reading took place in the yard of the State House on a platform used by David Rittenhouse as an observatory (which no longer existed in Rothermel's day).[1] Historian Benson Lossing described the Declaration being read to "a vast concourse of people gathered from the city and surrounding country."[2] With nearly seventy people represented (including Benjamin Franklin and an American Indian), Rothermel conveyed to his 1861 audience a sense of the far-reaching importance of the occasion.

The painting appeared at an auspicious moment: the nation, whose birth the picture celebrated, was tearing apart. Rothermel's depiction of the diverse crowd—women and men, young and old—about to be united by the Declaration of Independence was timely: As one contemporary put it: "The interest attaching to such a painting, particularly at such a time as this cannot be overestimated."[3] Rothermel likely aimed to tap the collective memory of American unity over division, most emphatically presented in the picture by his literal depiction of two comrades in arms. In his private life, his concern for national unity soon manifested itself in his private life too: he became a founding member of the Union League of Philadelphia, an organization committed to the preservation of nationhood. Five years later this painting was later presented to the Union League of Philadelphia by fellow member and art patron James L. Claghorn.

First Reading of the Declaration of Independence was exhibited at Dusseldorf Academy (New York) in 1861, Buffalo Fine Arts Academy in 1862, Rochester Academy of the Arts in 1862, and Philadelphia's Great Central Fair in 1867. The work entered the Union League collection in 1867.[4]

---

[1] "Our own Great Central Fair," *Our Daily Fare*, June 17, 1864, p. 69, found the work "marred somewhat by anachronism which, though slight, are still annoying to those who are hypercritical as regards the unities." The complaint concerned the inclusion of houses that would not have been in the background in 1776.

[2] Benson Lossing, *The Pictorial Field-Book of the Revolution* (New York: Harper Brothers, 1855), 2:81.

[3] Precisely when the artist finished the work is unknown, but he may have intended to complete it before July 4. A writer reported on January 21 that Rothermel was "working up" the composition ("Art Gossip," *New York Times*, January 21, 1861, p. 2).

[4] Besides the title given here, the work was exhibited as *1776—Reading the Declaration of Independence*, *Reading the Declaration of Independence*, and *Reading the Declaration*.

Study of a Child for Christian Martyrs in the Coliseum

Cat. 18
Study of a Child for
Christian Martyrs in the Coliseum
1862
Inscribed lower right:
  P. F. Rothermel / 1862
Oil on canvas, 24 × 20 inches
(61 × 50.8 cm)
Bowdoin College Museum of Art,
Brunswick, Maine; gift of
Mrs. John H. Halford in memory
of John H. Halford '07

For a time this painting was thought to depict one of Rothermel's sons; however, in 1862 his youngest was twelve years old. While the child is unidentified, the composition is recognizably related to Rothermel's famous *Christian Martyrs in the Coliseum* (1862–63, unlocated).

This fully developed study focuses on the child found in the lower right section of the large painting but not in the compositional sketch (cat. 18a). Describing the "noble group" to which the child belongs in the larger painting, the Reverend Henry J. Morton of Philadelphia's Saint James (Episcopal) Church wrote: "In deadly fear a mother has swooned, and her little infant, all unconscious, smiles as it sits beside her."[1] In contrast, in the study the child displays a serious countenance, not an uncomprehending smile.

That Rothermel signed and dated this piece suggests that he regarded it as an exhibitable work of art. Another of his studies, the head of a martyr, was included in the 1863 Pennsylvania Academy of the Fine Arts annual exhibition. Listed with John T. Tait as owner, that work is surely the signed and dated (1862) painting of a female martyr now in the museum of the Pennsylvania Academy of the Fine Arts.[2] Both it and this study of the child display the same high degree of finish.

[1] Henry J. Morton, "Mr. Rothermel's New Picture, *Christian Martyrs in the Coliseum*" (Philadelphia, 1863), p. 3. The pamphlet (HSP) was published in connection with the exhibition of the painting at the Pennsylvania Academy.

[2] Caroline Gibson Taitt gave the work to the academy.

Study for Christian Martyrs in the Coliseum

Cat. 18a
Study for *Christian Martyrs in the Coliseum*
ca. 1862
Ink and wash on paper,
9 5/8 × 7 1/4 inches
(24.4 × 18.4 cm)
Gil E. Pablo, M.D. Collection

This compositional drawing is for Rothermel's *Christian Martyrs in the Coliseum* (1862–63, unlocated), deemed the artist's greatest achievement by many contemporaries, including Henry T. Tuckerman in his important 1867 book on American art:

> To say that it is Mr. Rothermel's best painting is to compliment it very highly...none [of his earlier work] boasted so much beauty and possessed so little blemish. It is in composition and color that Mr. Rothermel, by common consent, is admitted to excel, and his composition was never finer, his color never more pure and charming. Upon this large canvas, with this noble subject, he has had ample opportunity to use all the resources of his genius. He has never chosen a better subject, or treated one with more energy and elaboration.[1]

"One of the chief attractions of the Art Gallery" of Philadelphia's Great Central Fair (1864), the large painting also "attracted much attention at the Centennial Exhibition."[2] The picture also appeared in other venues—Boston Athenaeum (1864, 1868–70), Pittsburgh Art Association (1870–71), and an American art exhibition in London (1887). Its renown was furthered by a photographic carte (3 1/2 × 2 7/16 inches) printed by Frederick Debourg Richards in 1863 (fig. 19).

While the ink drawing conveys a sense of detail, the loosely applied lines and washes suggest a sketch quickly rendered. Its figural arrangement closely anticipates the finished painting but includes only half the foreground figures and not the child in the lower right (see cat. 18). Further, in the fully realized *Christian Martyrs in the Coliseum*, Rothermel expanded the architectural setting, showed the elevated soldier gesturing dynamically toward the arena, and moved the standing woman from shadow to light. Accordingly, the drawing represents an early stage in the development of the painting.[3]

[1] Henry T. Tuckerman, *Book of the Artists* (1867; reprint, New York: James F. Carr, 1966), p. 438.

[2] "Our Own Great Central Fair," *Our Daily Fare*, June 17, 1864, 69; Clara Erkstine Clement, "Early Religious Painting in America," *New England Magazine* 11 (December 1894): 401.

[3] The Pennsylvania Academy of the Fine Arts also owns an ink compositional drawing.

Fig. 19 Frederick Debourg Richards
Photograph carte, 3 3/4 × 2 7/16 in.
Private collection

State House on the Day of the Battle of Germantown

Cat. 19
State House on the Day of the Battle of Germantown
Inscribed lower right:
  P. F. Rothermel 1862
Oil on canvas,
34 1/2 × 47 1/2 inches
(87.6 × 120.6)
Museum of American Art of the Pennsylvania Academy of the Fine Arts, Philadelphia; bequest of Henry C. Gibson

The idea for the subject of this 1862 painting probably dates to 1856, when Rothermel asked Robert C. Davis for any engravings of officers wounded at the Battle of Germantown.[1] Indeed, among the commissions that he received prior to his August 1856 departure for Europe is "Thos. Allibone, Evening of the Battle of Germantown State House" for $500.[2] Rothermel copied into notebook two passages pertaining to the Battle of Germantown taken from John F. Watson's *Annals of Philadelphia*. The longer reads:

> The day of the Battle of Germantown we heard firing all day. But knew not the result towards evening they brought the wounded the Prisoners were carried to the State House lobbies and the street was presently filled with women [taking lint] and bandages and every refreshment which they thought their suffering country men might want.[3]

Also in the notebook, under "Munich 1859," he wrote:

> L. W. Broadwell of New Orleans has ordered a Picture of the day of the Battle of Germantown—scene before the State House Philad. The Rebel Ladies succouring the wounded. As per—note received this day, Jan 10, 1859, Munich.[4]

What became of the paintings commissioned by Allibone and Broadwell, if actually executed, is unknown. It is also not clear who (if anyone) commissioned this 1862 composition; however, Henry C. Gibson owned it the following year, when it was exhibited at the National Academy of Design with the title, *Revolutionary Patriotism:—Front of the State House, Philadelphia, on the day of the Battle of Germantown, October 4, 1777*. The picture was also included in the 1864 Great Central Fair in Philadelphia.[5]

At the latter venue the painting received attention in the fair's newspaper: "the artist has succeeded in making a very effective grouping, and of conveying a very excellent idea of such a scene at such an era, and under such circumstances." The painting was marred by a slight anachronism that did not affect its merit as a work of art, "but the picture would please us better if the main door of the old building had been painted as it was in 1776, and not as it was made many years afterwards by some vandalish city commissioner, who desire to make a 'job' for a political favorite."[6] Despite this flaw, Rothermel's rendering of the State House served its purpose by convincingly siting the scene.

Not a battle painting in the traditional sense, *State House on the Day of the Battle of Germantown* shows the aftermath of and casualties resulting from the October 4, 1777, conflict. Arranged around the center of the composition are groups of women tending to wounded soldiers. The picture also includes a variety of figures—including British soldiers, wounded Americans, children, a

scout in buckskins, an African American woman, and gentlemen—who evince a wide range of physical and mental states. In bringing soldiers and civilians—men, women and children—together, Rothermel expressed the deadly impact, suffering, and confusion of war, as well as its attendant acts of comforting and nursing. The image of women as merciful agents providing aid likely resonated with the Civil War audience.

The Great Central Fair benefited the United States Sanitary Commission, a civilian relief agency aiding Union troops and in which women assumed vital roles. Given the importance of female participation in the Sanitary Commission, along with the painting's venue and subject, *State House on the Day of the Battle of Germantown* can be read as authorizing the significant efforts of contemporary women by connecting them to hallowed Revolutionary counterparts. Whether or not Rothermel intended this linkage, his painting presented a timely and appropriate image for the Great Central Fair.

[1] P. F. Rothermel to Robert C. Davis, July 24, 1856, Charles Roberts Collection, Autographs of American Artists, Haverford College Library. Rothermel was interested mainly in obtaining from what he called Davis's "Collection of Revolutionary worthies" engravings of 22 persons, almost entirely women, that he listed in the letter. He identifies some as being "The Ladies of the 'Meschcensa,' " by which he means the "Meschianza." This was a lavish farewell party—featuring a medieval-like tournament—organized by John Andre for Gen. William Howe on May 18, 1878. The "Ladies" were Philadelphia belles invited to this British event. Apparently, Rothermel intended to paint this. In his notebook, a similar list appears under the heading "Blendid Rose," one of the two teams of "knights" (the other, "Burning Mountain," is also on this list). John F. Watson, *Annals of Philadelphia, and Pennsylvania in the Olden Time* (1857; rev. ed., Philadelphia: Edwin S. Stuart, 1899), 2: facing 290, provides an illustration of the tournament. Watson's book was well known to Rothermel, as evidenced by his notebook.

[2] Peter F. Rothermel notebook.

[3] Rothermel's source is Watson, *Annals*, 2:285. His other excerpt comes from p. 287: "After Battle of Germantown officers who were [made] Prisoners were confined days on an upper room of the State House, afterward Peales Museum." Rothermel's transcription deviates slightly, but insignificantly, from the original.

[4] The same description from the notebook—"Battle of Germantown/Scene before the State House Philad."—is inscribed on a sheet with a sketch of the three standing women with others around them (private collection).

[5] After Gibson's death, his collection passed to the Pennsylvania Academy of the Fine Arts. Author Helen Henderson (*The Pennsylvania Academy of the Fine Arts and other Collections of Philadelphia* [Boston: L. C. Page, 1911], p. 187) described the Gibson collection and the work of the three Americans—Gilbert Stuart, Thomas Sully, and Rothermel—represented in it, and then dismissed Rothermel's art: "His style was photographic and his colour suggests the chromo, but he was at one time much in vogue as an exponent of the sentimental, the tragic and the pathetic in art."

[6] "Our Own Great Central Fair," *Our Daily Fare*, June 17, 1864, p. 69. Rothermel's rendering of the window architraves and classical elements around the door are also probably those of 1862, not 1777. The building underwent modifications in the nineteenth century, and an 1876 engraving shows a entrance similar to Rothermel's; see Edward M. Riley, "The Independence Hall Group," in "Historic Philadelphia from the Founding until the Early Nineteenth Century," *Transactions of the American Philosophical Society* 43 (1953): 37. Various eighteenth-century engravings demonstrate that the original door treatment was much simpler; see, for example, Benson J. Lossing, *The Pictorial Field-Book of the Revolution* (New York: Harper & Brothers, 1855), p. 66.

The Last Sigh of the Moor

Cat. 20
The Last Sigh of the Moor
Inscribed lower left:
  P. F. Rothermel 1864
Oil on canvas,
47 15/16 × 72 inches
(121.8 × 182.9 cm)
Museum of American Art of
the Pennsylvania Academy of
the Fine Arts, Philadelphia;
gift of Caroline Gibson Taitt

Rothermel took his theme from Washington Irving's *Chronicle of the Conquest of Granada*. This popular book appeared in 1829, a year after Irving's *History of the Life and Voyages of Christopher Columbus*, which had served Rothermel as the source for *Columbus before the Queen* (see cat. 2). Unlike the more scholarly *Columbus*, Irving's *Granada* was purposely a romantic blend of fact and fiction. Indeed, the author wrote the American edition under the pseudonym Fray Antonio Agapida, "allowing me" he wrote his publisher "a freer scope in touching up and coloring the subject from my imagination."[1] Irving's attitude is clearly parallel to Rothermel's approach to art and suggests why the painter was drawn to this author.

A dramatically romantic image, *The Last Sigh of the Moor* shows the King Boabdil and his retinue in retreat, pausing to gaze back over Granada, which has fallen to Ferdinand and Isabella. In its mixture of the exotic and the tragic, the composition recalls and seems to combine elements of Theodore Gericuault's *Raft of the Medusa* (1819) and Eugene Delacroix's *Scenes from the Massacre at Chios* (1824) and *Death of Saranapalus* (1827). Delacroix was an artist Rothermel especially admired ("Of all the Colour I have yet seen Delacroix is the best of the moderns"); however, the painting primarily owes its form to Irving's account.[2]

Near the end of the book, in chapter 99 "Surrender of Granada," Rothermel found his subject:

> At two leagues' distance the cavalcade winding into the skirts of the the Alpuxarras, ascended an eminence commanding the last view of Granada. As they arrived at this spot the Moors paused involuntarily to take a farewell gaze at their beloved city, which in a few steps more, would shut from their sight forever. Never had it appeared so lovely in their eyes. The sunshine, so bright in that transparent climate, lit up each tower and minaret, and rested gloriously upon the crowning battlements of the Alhambra, while the vega spread its enamelled bosom of verdure below, glistening with the silver windings of the Xenel. The Moorish cavaliers gazed with a silent agony of tenderness and grief, upon that delicious abode, the scene of their loves and pleasures. While they yet looked, a light cloud of smoke burst forth from the citadel, and presently a peal of artillery, faintly heard, told that the city was taken possession of, and the throne of the Moslem Kings was lost for ever.... The unhappy monarch...was not to be consoled, his tears continued to flow. "Allah Achbar!" exclaimed he. "When did misfortunes ever equal mine!"

> From this circumstance the hill which is not far from Padul took the name of Feg Allah Achbar; but the point of view commanding the last prospect of Granada, is known among Spaniards by the name of *el ultimo suspiro del Moro*, or "the last sigh of the Moor."[3]

Although Rothermel eschewed the bright sunshine mentioned in the passage for the more emotionally poignant setting sun, he otherwise remained true to the spirit of his source.

A negative review soon appeared in the *Round Table*, a New York publication that typically regarded Rothermel's work in an unfavorable light. The writer termed the composition hurriedly finished and noted, disagreeably, that "many of the characters we have come to recognize and look on as old friends in Mr. Rothermel's pictures. There is the same gray-headed man with the child leaning against his knee that we have seen in the 'Christian Martyrs' and other works."[4] The observation about the familiarity of Rothermel's "characters" is valid, for his figures often portray types—rather than individuals—that recur in his compositions; however, given his adherence to the academic tradition of valuing the general over the specific, this is not a surprising occurence. *The Last Sigh of the Moor* faithfully, and grandly, visualizes the pageantry, loss, and melancholia of Irving's account.

[1] Earl N. Harbert and Miriam Shillingsburg, *A Chronicle of the Conquest of Granada by Fray Antonio Agapida* (Boston: Twayne Publishers, 1988), p. xx.

[2] [Probably 1856,] Rothermel notebook.

[3] Harbert and Shillingsburg, *Chronicle*, pp. 290–91. The work is listed in the catalogue for the 1864 annual exhibition at the Pennsylvania Academy as *L'Ultimo Surpiro del Moro* owned by J. T. Tait.

[4] L., "Art—Philadelphia Art Notes," *Round Table*, May 7, 1864, p. 327.

"Look at Dolly"

Cat. 21
"Look at Dolly"
1864
Oil on paper, 5 × 3 inches
(12.7 × 7.6 cm)
The Historical Society of
Delaware

Just a few years prior to gaining a commission for one of the largest paintings in the United States, Rothermel executed one of the smallest: *"Look at Dolly"* was featured in the Model House at the Great Central Fair in Philadelphia. The house, designed by the architects Edward Collins and C. M. Autenrieth, was minutely and exquisitely detailed. As *Our Daily Fare*, the newspaper of the fair, reported:

> The building is divided into three stories, and each room is complete with miniature furniture. The book case contains volumes suited to the Lilliputian character of the establishment. The "Art Gallery" is the crowning feature. At the door there is supposed to be sold a catalogue of the collection of Paintings. The size of the book is in keeping with the building. The title page reads:

> Price, 1 mill.
>
> Catalogue
> of the
> Grildrig Collection
> of
> Pictures
> Lately imported from the Kingdom of Lilliput,
> and exhibiting for the
> Benefit of the
> Great Central Fair.[1]

Twenty-six paintings formed the collection. Aside from Rothermel, the best known artist was James Hamilton, who had three works included. All the tiny pictures were given gilded frames by Earles' Galleries of Philadelphia.[2] Sixteen of the paintings remain in the house today.

Rothermel's depiction of a child holding her doll contrasts in every way with the large number of big paintings he then had on exhibition at the same fair, including *Christ and the Doctors* (cat. 16) and *State House on the Day of the Battle of Germantown* (cat. 19).

[1] "The Model House," *Our Daily Fare*, June 13, 1864, p. 38.

[2] Anne S. Woodward, " 'Miniature Mansion': The Model House at the Historical Society of Delaware," *Delaware Antiques Show* (Wilmington, Del., 1990), p. 67.

The Bather

Cat. 22
The Bather
Inscribed lower left:
  P. F. Rothermel / 1865
Oil on canvas,
16³/₄ by 10⁹/₁₆ inches
(42.5 × 26.8 cm)
Museum of American Art of
the Pennsylvania Academy
of the Fine Arts, Philadelphia;
bequest of Henry C. Gibson

Fig. 20 Peter Frederick Rothermel, *The Bather*,
1865, oil on canvas. Joseph Szymanski, Pasadena,
California

One of two nearly identical versions, this painting belonged to Henry C. Gibson, who collected other Rothermels, including *De Soto Raising the Cross on the Banks of the Mississippi* (cat. 7), *State House on the Day of the Battle of Germantown* (cat. 19), *Desdemona* (cat. 24), and *Queen Elizabeth Signing the Death Warrant of Essex* (unlocated). Hector Tyndale owned the other version of *The Bather* (fig. 20).[1] Both paintings depict a reclining idealized female nude who languidly dangles her foot in water. A large urn and some trees appear in the background (more clearly so in the Tyndale version). The same sinuous twist of the body characterizes both pictures, but here the figure's right arm rests slightly higher and she has raised her left arm as though to shield her eyes from the sun as she looks in our direction. In the other painting, the woman's raised arm goes behind her head and, with eyes down, she appears passive and lost in thought. Though minor, these differences do affect our interaction with the paintings. With the Tyndale figure, we assume the familiar role of viewer-as-voyeur; the Gibson version encourages a more active involvement between us and the steady gaze of the nude.

The Bather belongs to the long history of idealized female nudes. To enter into this tradition an academic artist like Rothermel devoted much time to drawing the live model and studying various images for compositional inspiration. His life drawings, often about the same size as this painting, show realistically rendered models in poses derived from the idealized tradition (cat. 39). As a fine example of this academic process, *The Bather* resembles numerous paintings that Rothermel would have known through reproductions and exhibitions. Certainly one obvious general source is John Vanderlyn's *Ariadne* (1814), a work then in the collection of Rothermel's patron and friend, Joseph Harrison, Jr. Unlike that grand history painting with its inflated figure, the much smaller *The Bather* presents a quieter sensibility that some people preferred. (For example, when praising another small work [probably *The Soldier's Widow*] a critic noted, "[The artist] has fortunately spared us the grand historical, and painted a simple little picture of a single figure, which has really a great deal of feeling....We feel more grateful to this artist for this little scene of poverty than for all his gorgeous Moors and Romans."[2] *The Bather* similarly demonstrates the artist's ability to create an appealingly intimate work, without pageantry and drama.

[1] Tyndale's painting now belongs to Joseph Szymanski, Pasadena, Calif. Its dimensions are virtually the same and it, too, is signed and dated in the lower left. It was shown at the Pennsylvania Academy of the Fine Arts' annual exhibition in 1865 and at Philadelphia's Union League Club in 1873 and, apparently, 1874. An unidentified clipping ("The Fine Arts," [1874], "Newspaper Clippings," book, p. 7, Papers of James Lawrence Claghorn, Archives of American Art, Smithsonian Institution) mentions Rothermel's "fair example of the nude, called 'The Bather', belonging to General Hector Tyndale." One of the two was also exhibited at the Philadelphia Sketch Club in December 1865; however, since a owner was not cited in the catalogue, it is unclear which version this was.

[2] L., "Art—Philadelphia Art Notes," *Round Table*, June 18, 1864, p. 10.

Study for Origin of the Guelph and Ghibelline War

Cat. 23
Study for *Origin of the Guelph and Ghibelline War*
ca. 1864–1865
Inscribed lower right:
  P. F. Rothermel
Oil on canvas,
24 1/2 × 18 inches
(62.2 × 45.7 cm)
Descendant of P.F. Rothermel

Of the six Rothermel paintings in the 1865 annual exhibition of the Pennsylvania Academy of the Fine Arts, Edwin Fitler, a prominent manufacturer who later became mayor of Philadelphia, owned two: *Lady Macbeth* and *Origin of the Guelph and Ghibelline War* (both unlocated). It is to the latter painting that this oil study is linked.

While no description of the painting exists, the Pennsylvania Academy catalogue entry included an excerpt from Simonde de Sismondi's *History of the Italian Republics*:

> Buondelmonte a Guelph noble of Florence, demanded in marriage a daughter of the house of "Amidei," a Ghibelline. While the nuptials were in progress a noble lady of the "Donati" stopped the bridegroom as he was passing her door, and bringing him into a room where her women were at work, unveiled her daughter, saying, "This is the wife I had reserved for you. Like you, she is a Guelph." Buondelmonte accepted her hand. The Amidei looked upon his inconsistency as a deep affront. The "Ghibelline" faction met and determined he should atone for the offence. Buondelmonte was attacked on Easter Sunday, just as he had crossed the "Ponte Vecchio," and killed. The Guelphs retaliated. And thus began the wars of the Guelphs and Ghibellines.[1]

Traditionally, 1216 is given as date of this event.

Rothermel's oil study, which shows a lessening of finish from the right side to the left, presents a scene of confusion and violence. In the center, one figure attacks another with a sword, while behind them riders are locked in combat. Bodies lie in a street confined by a jumble of towering buildings (an effect enhanced by the vertical format). In the lower right, a man energetically points out the action to a well-dressed woman leaning on a barrel. On the opposite side, figures appear to be rushing to a church. A scampering dog, in the lower center, adds to the chaos of the moment. Further compositional movement results from Rothermel's strategic placement of his characteristic glowing orangish-red hue.

Although the action in the oil study is not entirely clear, what is represented, coupled with the medieval, Italianate costumes and architecture, does support the notion that the work relates to the *Origin of the Guelph and Ghibelline War*.

[1] *Catalogue of the Forth-First Annual Exhibition of the Pennsylvania Academy of the Fine Arts* (Philadelphia, 1865), p. 17. Jean-Charles-Lionard Simonde de Sismondi's multivolume work was published in France from 1807 to 1818. English editions began appearing in the United States in 1832. Politically the Guelphs were aligned with the Pope, and the Ghibellines with the German Holy Roman Emperor.

99

Desdemona

Cat. 24
Desdemona
1865
Oil on canvas,
11 3/16 × 8 1/16 inches
(28.4 × 20.5 cm)
Museum of Americn Art of
the Pennsylvania Academy
of the Fine Arts, Philadelphia;
bequest of Henry C. Gibson

Rothermel offered a small, intimate study of Shakespeare's heroine lost in thought, with what appears to be a sword near her elbow resting on a table. The artist depicted not a specific scene in *Othello*, but rather conflated episodes: the swordplay following Desdemona's death; the Moor's reference to Desdemona as "my fair warrior"; and the heroine's pleading before the Venetian Senate to accompany her husband to Cyprus:

> That I did love the Moor to live with him,
> My dowright violence and storm of fortunes
> May trumpet to the world. My heart's subdued
> Even to the very quality of my lord....
> So that, dear lords, if I be left behind
> A moth of peace, and he go to war,
> The rites for which I love him are bereft me,
> And I a heavy interim shall support
> By his dear absence. Let me go with him.[1]

Broadly painted, the work—termed a "little gem" by one contemporary—displays an almost sketchlike freshness.[2] It was shown at the First Annual Prize Exhibition of the Philadelphia Sketch Club in December 1865, and it appeared in the Pennsylvania Academy of Fine Arts annual exhibition of 1866, at which point it was owned by M. W. Baldwin. The following year a *Desdemona* exhibited at the Rhode Island Society for Domestic Industry belonged to Albert Dailey. Presumably the Baldwin picture is the one later owned by Henry C. Gibson that passed to the Pennsylvania Academy of the Fine Arts, and the Dailey painting is the version of nearly identical size that is today in a private collection.

Desdemona is one of approximately twenty paintings that Rothermel rendered of Shakespearean subjects.[3] Stylistically speaking, the painting resembles the work of Charles Robert Leslie and Thomas Sully, both of whom painted numerous Shakespearean subjects. Rothermel's similarities to Sully were recognized about the time he painted *Desdemona*: "Mr. Sully still remains as a golden link in the chain that connects the art of today with that of the past, and with him are associated Rothermel...."[4]

[1] Norman Sanders, ed., *Othello* (Cambridge: Cambridge University Press, 1984), act 2, scene 1, line 173 and act 1, scene 3, lines 244–47, 251–55. I appreciate Marjorie Lewis's thoughtful observations on this painting.

[2] "Art—Philadelphia Art Notes," *Round Table*, May 5, 1866, p. 279.

[3] For a listing of Rothermel's Shakespearean subjects, see Richard Studing, *Shakespeare in American Painting: A Catalogue from the Late Eighteenth Century to the Present* (Rutherford, N.J.: Fairleigh Dickinson University Press, 1993), pp. 117–18.

[4] "The Artists' Fund Society," *New Age*, March 22, 1867, p. 2.

Sharpshooters at Round Top

Cat. 25
Sharpshooters at Round Top
Inscribed lower right:
  P. F. Rothermel / 1867
Oil on canvas,
$24^1/_2 \times 29$ inches
(62.2 $\times$ 73.7 cm)
The State Museum of
Pennsylvania, PHMC

This is one of several paintings related to Rothermel's immense *The Battle of Gettysburg: Pickett's Charge*, commissioned by the Commonwealth of Pennsylvania in 1866. A fine painting in its own right, *Sharpshooters at Round Top* can also be understood as a stage in the development of the huge composition as well as an outstanding example of Rothermel's research as he studied various aspects and pictorial possibilities of the three-day long battle. Unlike the overwhelming breadth characterizing *The Battle of Gettysburg: Pickett's Charge*, this compositon narrows the focus to a few men fighting on the rocky hill known as Little Round Top.[1]

Although the title simply cites "Round Top," both a Big and a Little Round Top exist. In terms of the overall battle, Little Round Top held greater strategic importance, and fierce fighting occurred on it during the second day of battle, July 2, 1863. That Rothermel had Little Round Top firmly in mind is supported by the rocky terrain: this hill had been cleared recently, while Big Round Top was still quite wooded. (Another of his paintings, *Charge of the Pennsylvania Reserves at Plum Run* [fig. 21], offers a different angle of vision on the two Round Tops and shows their distinctive characteristics.)[2]

Fig. 21 Peter Frederick Rothermel, *Charge of the Pennsylvania Reserves at Plum Run* (from the Confederates' side), c. 1868, oil on canvas, 25 $^1/_2 \times$ 60 in. The State Museum of Pennsylvania, Pennsylvania Historical and Museum Commission

Rothermel's picture convincingly conveys the noise, heat, and confusion of the action and even seems to anticipate a twentieth-century historian's description of what the soldiers faced on Little Round Top: "The air around them was sulfurous with smoke [and] underscored by the crash and rattle of musketry."[3] Intensely engaged in firing upon the enemy, these sharpshooters, whose successes and lives depend on their keen vision, see what we the viewers do not. And Rothermel depicted the sharpshooters differently from other artists, particularly Winslow Homer, who emphasized their cool detachment.[4] None of the sharpshooters in Rothermel's picture holds a telescopic rifle, their weapon of choice and symbol of their ability to rain death from a distance. On Rothermel's canvas, the sharpshooters are caught up in the thick of close-range fire.

Prominent among the riflemen is the dynamic standing figure wearing the exotic uniform of the Zouaves, who fought at Little Round Top.[5] The Zouave regiments (of which there were many on both sides) received attention for colorful garb derived from Algerian tribesmen by way of the French Army.[6] Their romantic outfits consisted of baggy red trousers, dark leggings with white gaiters, a short blue jacket with red trim, and a fez or soft cap. The prominent inclusion of the Zouaves allowed Rothermel to add color—especially his favorite, red—to an otherwise stony, smoky scene.

An inscription on the back of the canvas indicates that *Sharpshooters* was presented by the artist to Joseph Harrison, Jr, the prominent Philadelphian who was both patron and friend.[7] It was Harrison who spoke glowingly of the large *The Battle of Gettysburg: Pickett's Charge* and introduced the artist at the painting's gala unveiling at Philadelphia's Academy of Music on December 20, 1870. Harrison also lobbied to secure Rothermel's right to exhibit that painting privately before delivering it to the State Capitol in Harrisburg in mid 1871. Although it is not known when Rothermel gave *Sharpshooters at Round Top* to Harrison, the artist surely intended it as an appreciation of Harrison's ongoing support and as a token of their friendship.[8]

Just ten days before the unveiling of the larger picture, *Sharpshooters at Round Top* formed part of an exhibition at the Union League of Philadelphia.[9] No owner is listed in the accompanying catalogue, but both Harrison and Rothermel were members of the league, an organization begun in 1862 that was dedicated to the defense of the Union.[10]

[1] The painting has also been titled *Sharp Shooters* and *Zouave Sharpshooters at Gettysburg*.

[2] Mathew Brady's 1863 stereophotograph provides further supporting evidence; illustrated in William A. Frassanito, *Gettysburg: A Journey in Time* (New York: Charles Scribner's Sons, 1975), p. 164. Whether Rothermel saw this particular photograph is unknown, but given the renown of Brady's work and given Rothermel's intense research during this commission, he likely was familiar with it.

[3] Harry W. Pfanz, *Gettysburg: The Second Day* (Chapel Hill and London: University of North Carolina Press, 1987), p. 208. Pfanz provides a vividly detailed chapter on the fighting on Little Round Top.

[4] For an informative discussion of Homer and the image of the sharpshooter, see Christopher Kent Wilson, "Marks of Honor and Death: *Sharpshooter* and the Peninsula Campaign of 1862," in Marc Simpson et al., *Winslow Homer: Paintings of the Civil War* (San Francisco: Bedford Arts and Fine Arts Museums of San Francisco, 1988), pp. 25–45.

[5] Pfanz, *Gettysburg*, p. 228, state that the arrival of the 140th New York Zouave troops in newly issued uniforms "must have been a dramatic thing."

[6] The uniform first appeared in the Crimean War and was used by the French through the Franco-Prussian War of 1870. For art-related discussions of the Zouave uniform, see Marc Simpson, "The Brierwood Pipe," in Simpson et al. *Homer*, pp. 167–72, and Harold Holzer and Mark E. Neely, Jr., *Mine Eyes Have Seen the Glory: The Civil War in Art* (New York: Orion Books, 1993), pp. 281–82.

[7] Parke-Bernet Sale catalogue of February 20, 1963, lot 62, "Peter F. Rothermel," Artists' Files, New York Public Library.

[8] When the painting left Harrison's collection is unknown. It is not listed in the 1912 auction catalogue of the collection.

[9] James L. Yarnall and William H. Gerdts, *The National Museum of American Art's Index to American Art Exhibition Catalogues: From the Beginning through the 1876 Centennial Year* (Boston: G. K. Hall, 1986), 4:3060.

[10] Rothermel's name appears among the names on the original membership list. He became a member on January 12, 1863; Harrison was admitted on September 12, 1863. Rothermel had resigned from the league (on March 8, 1870) before this painting was exhibited there; see *Chronicle of the Union League of Philadelphia 1862 to 1902* (Philadelphia, 1902). The *Chronicle* cites the artist in its chapter entitled "Notable Men of the Union League": "There, too, was Peter Frederick Rothermel, the high-minded painter, in whose great picture of the Battle of Gettysburg are commemorated the supreme grandeur and the supreme agony of the war spirit in which the Union League was born" (p. 413).

Study for Battle of Gettysburg: Pickett's Charge

Cat. 26
Study for *Battle of Gettysburg: Pickett's Charge*
1867–1870
Inscribed lower center to right:
study [————] the [————]
line the / Battle of Gettysburg
Presented to the Keystone
Battery / through Capt.
Poulterer by P. F. Rothermel
Oil on canvas,
26 × 34 ½ inches
(66 × 87.6 cm)
Museum of Fine Arts, Boston;
bequest of Maxim Karolik

While carrying out the *Battle of Gettysburg* commission, Rothermel executed numerous studies of the battleground, soldiers, horses, and equipment. These works range from small, quickly penciled sketches (fig. 22) to more fully realized larger works, such as this painting.

Until recently, this composition, with its impressively rendered rearing horses, was thought to be by David Gilmour Blythe. The inscription, however, is in Rothermel's hand and the work is a study for the group on the left side of the huge *Battle of Gettysburg: Pickett's Charge* (see cat. 27).[1] In the final painting, part of the battery is obscured by Lieutenant Haskell announcing to Gen. George Meade (who in reality appeared on the scene later) that victory was at hand.[2]

From the inscription, one would assume that this painting was presented to the Keystone Battery in honor of their participation in the battle; however, that light artillery group, organized in Philadelphia on August 13, 1862, did not fight at Gettysburg.[3] The key to the larger painting identifies the group as Weir's Battery, a New York group. Lt. Gulian V. Weir commanded the 1st Regiment Light Artillery (Battery C) of the Fifth Army Corps, which saw intense action on July 3.

[1] I appreciate Bruce W. Chambers bringing this work to my attention.

[2] At the unveiling ceremony in Philadelphia's Academy of Music, Meade, responding to cheers for him to speak, praised the painting and acknowledged that its only error was his inclusion at the moment depicted (*Picture of the Battle of Gettysburg, Painted by P. F. Rothermel,* Philadelphia, 1871), p. 21.

[3] Keystone Battery joined the Army of the Potomac in pursuit of Lee after Gettysburg, fought at Wapping Heights, Va., and was mustered out on August 20, 1863. A second Keystone Battery was organized and served briefly in 1863. Matthew Hastings, who captained the battery, formed another battery in 1864. See Frederick H. Dyer, *A Compendium of the War of the Rebellion* (New York: Thomas Yoseloff, 1959), 3:1576. Stephen B. Poulterer served in the Keystone Battery; see *American Paintings in the Museum of Fine Arts, Boston* (Boston, 1969), 1:38. The Union League roster lists two other Poulterers (Edwin F. and William), who the artist, as a member, likely knew; see *Chronicle of the Union League of Philadelphia, 1862 to 1902* (Philadelphia, 1902), p. 508.

Fig. 22 [cat. 74] Study of a Soldier for *Battle of Gettysburg: Pickett's Charge,* 1867–1870
Gil E. Pablo, M.D. Collection

The Battle of Gettysburg: Pickett's Charge

Cat. 27
The Battle of Gettysburg:
Pickett's Charge
John Sartain after
Peter F. Rothermel
Copyright 1872, published 1879
Steel engraving and mezzotint,
24⁷/₈ × 38 ¹/₄ inches
(63.2 × 97.2 cm)
Amon Carter Museum, Fort
Worth; gift of Edward L. Mattil

This print reproduces the colossal battle painting unveiled at the Academy of Music in Philadelphia in 1870. Rothermel apparently conceived of producing an engraving in 1875; and informed James L. Claghorn, a patron and the president of the Pennsylvania Academy of the Fine Arts, indicating that he was considering commissioning John Sartain to execute a print "in his best style of line and stipple with a thin veil of mezzotint." Claghorn, who considered the picture "one of the finest Battle pieces coming under my notice," endorsed the idea.[1] Sartain considered it a "first rate opportunity" and described the plan to his daughter Emily: "[Rothermel] is to have a photographic copy of the picture made in four separate pieces, then to join these together and do the requisite touching along the lines of junction, and also add to the effect if necessary. From this or from a copy of this the plate to be engraved."[2]

The engraver's main concern was his ability to meet Rothermel's stipulation that the print be finished in time for the opening of the centennial exposition; on June 21, 1875, he agreed to the deadline and a $3000 fee.[3] The anxiety over the deadline owed to Sartain's appointment as Chair of the Bureau of Art for the exposition, and it was fully justified: the print was not ready by the opening. Rothermel was bitterly disappointed and his relations with Sartain remained decidedly cool for the next several years. In 1879 the artist maintained that he had expected Sartain to refuse the contract if there was the least doubt about finishing it on time but Sartain's "hankering after prominence proved too much for his honesty, and he accepted." Rothermel continued: "[Sartain's] word of honor is worthless until it seemed that it was easier and pleasanter for him to revel in the fanciful regions of fiction than the common prosaic truth. Had he been blessed with Imagination at all Equalling his conceded [conceited] qualities he could easily rivalled Homer."[4] Another contract was made on March 24, 1879, with the promise that the engraved steel plate was to be delivered in five days.[5]

Their difficulties finally behind them the two men apparently resumed friendly relations. Sartain included Rothermel's huge painting of the battle in an 1887 exhibition of American art held in London and, at the painter's death, spoke highly of him.

---

[1] Rothermel to Claghorn, April 19, 1875, and Claghorn to Rothermel, April 21, 1875, Kennedy Galleries, New York.

[2] Sartain to Emily Sartain, March 19, 1875 (begun December 20, 1874), Sartain Family Papers, HSP. Sartain indicated that the order for the plate had not yet been confirmed.

[3] Contract, Sartain Family Papers, HSP. The contract was witnessed by W. H. Macdowell, who was the father-in-law of Rothermel's daughter Blanche (also of Thomas Eakins).

[4] Rothermel Papers, Pennsylvania State Archives, Harrisburg. The date "January 7, 1879" appears in the margin of the second page of the manuscript.

[5] Contract, Sartain Family Papers, HSP. The delivery was to be made to the artist's son, Peter, Jr., a Philadelphia attorney.

Death of General Reynolds

Cat. 28
Death of General Reynolds
1870–1872
Oil on canvas, 36 × 66 inches
(91.4 × 167.6 cm)
The State Museum of
Pennsylvania, PHMC

This is one of four paintings, known as the "side series," executed to complement the huge *The Battle of Gettysburg: Pickett's Charge*.[1] The other three compositions are: *Repulse of the Louisiana Tigers, Charge of the Pennsylvania Reserves at Plum Run* (see fig. 21), and *Repulse of General Johnson's Division by General Geary's White Star Division*.[2] These smaller paintings, beginning with the *Death of General Reynolds*, chronicle episodes of the three-day battle of Gettysburg that culminated in Pickett's charge. Rothermel executed the side series after finishing the large painting in 1870, completing the entire commission—for which he received $25,000—by February 22, 1872. Surprisingly enough, the state had no adequate space to exhibit the works. At the urging of Joseph Harrison, Jr., they were hung as a group in a temporary gallery in Philadelphia's Fairmount Park, where they remained from 1873 to 1876, at which time the large painting was removed to Memorial Hall for the centennial exhibition and remained there for many years.[3] Finally, in 1894, all five paintings were installed in the new Library and Executive Building in Harrisburg.

Death of General Reynolds offers a scene that is episodic and realistic rather than focused and heroic. The composition centers on Union Army general, John Reynolds, who was struck down by a sharpshooter on the first day of the battle. But the artist treats the removal of the fallen officer as routine rather than momentous. Small figures, sketchily defined, engage in a variety of seemingly unrelated (and, thus, perhaps true-to-battle) actvities within a panoramic landscape. The impressive painterliness distinguishing the trees and smoke clouds display an ability in rendering landscape that makes it surprising Rothermel did not turn to the genre more often.

[1] Edwin B. Coddington, "Rothermel's Paintings of the Battle of Gettysburg," *Pennsylvania History* 27 (January 1960): 1–2.

[2] All four have nearly identical dimensions and are in the State Museum of Pennsylvania; for reproductions see Donald A. Winer, "Rothermel's Battle of Gettysburg: A Victorian's Heroic View of the Civil War," *Nineteenth Century* 1 (Winter 1975): 6–10. In 1881 Rothermel completed a larger version of the *Charge of the Pennsylvania Reserves* (State Museum of Pennsylvania), which depicts the scene from the Confederate lines instead of the Union lines.

[3] Harrison had long wanted to establish a free art gallery in Philadelphia; see Sue Himelick Nutty, "Joseph Harrison, Jr. (1810–1874): Philadelphia Art Collector," Ph.D. diss., University of Delaware, 1993, 1:281–84.

The Bride of Lammermoor

Cat. 29
The Bride of Lammermoor
Inscribed lower left:
  P. F. Rothermel / 1873
Oil on canvas, 36 × 43 inches
(91.4 × 109.2 cm)
Woodmere Art Museum;
gift of Miss Margaret Banes, 1950

This is one of several Rothermel paintings illustrating episodes from Sir Walter Scott's phenomenally popular Waverley novels. Among the others are: *Death of Old Mortality* (ca. 1841, unlocated), *John Balfour of Burley in the Cave* (see cat. 52), *Sir Walter Raleigh and Queen Elizabeth* (1854, private collection), *Queen Elizabeth at Kenilworth Castle* (ca. 1868, private collection), *Rose Bradwardine* (ca. 1855, unlocated), and *Lucy Ashton and Ravenswood at the Spring* (ca. 1849, unlocated). The last, like this painting, derives from Scott's 1819 tragedy *The Bride of Lammermoor*.

This historical romance may have particularly appealed to Rothermel because Scott presented the tale as if taken from the notes of one Dick Tinto, an artist who, like Rothermel, began his career as a sign painter. In the novel's "Preliminary," Tinto displays a sketch for a large painting:

> [A] female figure of exquisite beauty,…in an attitude of speechless terror, appeared to watch the issue of a debate betwixt two other persons. The one was a young man, in the Vandyke dress common to the time of Charles I., who, with an air of indignant pride, testified by the manner in which he raised his head and extended his arm, seemed to be urging a claim of right, rather than of favor, to a daly, whose age, and some resemblance in their features, pointed her out as the mother of the younger female.[1]

Since the painting captures the confrontational spirit of this sketch, we can imagine that Rothermel saw himself as realizing Tinto's composition.

Like many Rothermel paintings, *The Bride of Lammermoor* focuses on a moment fraught with action and reaction. The scene shows Edgar, Master of Ravenswood, surprising the group that has just witnessed Lucy Ashton sign her wedding contract with Hayston of Bucklaw. Lucy, having abandoned hope of marrying Ravenswood, has dropped her pen and "seemed stiffened to stone." Bucklaw, in his splendid red costume, stands "haughty and with affected indifference." Captain Craigengelt prepares to draw his sword, while the Presbyterian minister, Mr. Bide-the-Bent and Lady Ashton react with shock and concern. On the left side of the composition sits Lord Ashton with his son Col. Douglas Ashton behind him. In the doorway appear two domestics "transfixed with surprise."[2] In the picture's center, with his back to the viewer and sword drawn, stands Ravenswood.

Rothermel's colorful depiction dramatically visualizes chapter 32:

> [Ravenswood] planted himself full in the middle of the apartment, opposite the table at which Lucy was seated.…His dark-colored riding cloak, displaced from one shoulder, hung around one side of his person in the ample folds of the Spanish mantle.…His slouched hat, which he had not removed at entrance, gave an additional gloom to his dark

features, which wasted by sorrow…added to a countenance naturally somewhat stern and wild a fierce and even savage expression….He said not a single word, and there was a deep silence in the company for more than two minutes.

Rothermel subtly expanded the narrative by including a portrait above Ravenswood's head, undoubtedly that of Edgar's ancestor, Sir Malise Ravenswood. Earlier in Scott's story, young Henry Ashton is filled with foreboding when he perceives a resemblance between this portrait and Edgar. Later, after the episode Rothermel depicts, the portrait mysteriously appears on the walls of the bridal ballroom and "seemed to frown wrath and vengeance upon the party assembled below." Rothermel's strategic inclusion of this portrait both enlarged the narrative and asserted the affective power of images, a quality Rothermel certainly embraced in his art.

Whether *The Bride of Lammermoor* was comissioned is unknown, but it did enter the important Joseph Harrison collection.

[1] Walter Scott, *Waverley Novels* (New York: Collier Publishers, n.d.), 4:326.

[2] These quotations and the extract that follows are from Scott, *Waverley Novels*, 4:453, 454, 400.

(Cat. 30)

Lady Dedlock Leaving Tulkinghorn

Cat. 30
Lady Dedlock Leaving Tulkinghorn
1884
Inscribed on back:
  Lady Dedlock leaving
  Tulkinghorn / close of Interview
  in his / turret chamber
  [?] / vide / Dickens /
  Bleak House / P.F. Rothermel /
  1884 / LimerickSta. /
  Montgomery Co/Pa/[in anoth-
  er hand?] CHAPTER
  XLI/BLEAK HOUSE
Oil on canvas,
25 × 12 ½ inches
(63.5 × 31.8 cm)
Raymond and Diane Waltz

During the artist's last ten years, ill health and cataracts limited his work. *Lady Dedlock Leaving Tulkinghorn* was his last "serious" painting, in the sense that he intended it for exhibition. No later paintings are known, and it was the last one he sent to a Pennsylvania Academy of the Fine Arts annual exhibition (1888). That contemporaries later realized the composition was his final significant work is implied in an obituary: "It is characteristic of the painter that he has never aimed at technical effects only, for all his pictures from 'Columbus Embarking at Palos' to 'Lady Dedlock' have a literary purport."[1] Bracketing a forty-year period, these two paintings delimit Rothermel's career. *Lady Dedlock Leaving Tulkinghorn* demonstrates the artist's unwavering commitment to narrative painting in the grand manner, even in a small canvas.

Charles Dickens's *Bleak House* provided the subject for the painting. Rothermel depicts the sinister legal adviser Tulkinghorn threatening to reveal a secret he has discovered about Lady Honoria Dedlock. The painter succeeded in representing the episode by conveying the essential qualities of these two antagonists. Early in the novel Dickens described them both. Lady Dedlock arrived with "beauty, pride, ambition, insolent resolve, and sense enough to portion out a legion of fine ladies. Wealth and station, added to these, soon floated her upward; and for years, now, my Lady Dedlock has been at the centre of the fashionable intelligence, and at the top of the fashionable tree." Tulkinghorn, on the other hand, is an "old gentleman, rusty to look at."[2] Rothermel set the haughty elegance of the woman off against the malevolence of the shadowy lawyer, not only by contrasting facial expressions, but also by juxtaposing freely applied paint to rich atmospheric tones.

Lady Dedlock Leaving Tulkinghorn was one of nine Rothermel paintings included in the American art exhibition at Earl's Court, London, in 1887.

[1] "Artist Rothermel Died," *Reading Weekly Eagle*, August 24, 1895, p. 1. My thanks to Holly K. Green for providing me with this article. "Columbus Embarking at Palos" must be *Embarkation of Columbus* (ca. 1844, unlocated).

[2] Charles Dickens, *Bleak House* (Oxford: Oxford University Press, 1987), pp. 10, 11.

God's Covenant with Noah

Cat. 31
God's Covenant with Noah
John Sartain after
Peter F. Rothermel
1847
Engraving, 4 3/8 × 5 7/8 inches
(11.1 × 14.9 cm)
Published in H. Hastings Weld,
Scenes in the Lives of the Patriarchs and Prophets (Philadelphia: Lindsay & Blakiston, 1847), p. 44.
Moore College of Art and Design, Permanent Collection

Philadelphia was an important publishing center, and in the 1840s and 1850s engravings after Rothermel drawings and paintings appeared in various journals and gift books. The years 1847 and 1848 especially saw a number of these appear before the public. His subject matter in these illustrations continued the historical themes of his grand paintings. This particular illustration appeared in *Scenes in the Lives of the Patriarchs and Prophets.*

The composition shows Noah after the Flood, when he "built an altar to the LORD, and took of every clean animal and every clean bird, and offered burnt offerings on the altar" (Genesis 9:20). The ark rests in the distance, and a great rainbow crowns the sky. The image appeared opposite an anonymous poem titled: "The Bow in the Cloud," which opened with an epigram taken from Genesis 9:11–13:

And I will establish my convenant with you; neither shall all flesh be cut off any more by the waters of a flood; neither shall there any more be a flood to destroy the earth.

And God said, this *is* the token of the convenant which I make between me and you and every living creature that *is* with you, for perpetual generations.

I do set my Bow in the cloud, and it shall be a token of a convenant between me and the earth.

Froissart and Queen Philippa

Cat. 32
Froissart and Queen Philippa
John Sartain after
Peter F. Rothermel
1848
Engraving, $6\frac{3}{8}$ × $5\frac{1}{4}$ inches
(16.2 × 13.3 cm)
Published in John Sartain, ed.,
*The American Gallery of Art: From
the Works of the Best Artists, with
Poetical and Prose Illustrations, by
Distinguished American Authors*
(Philadelphia: Lindsay &
Blakiston, 1848), frontis.
Moore College of Art and
Design, Permanent Collection

The American Gallery of Art was intended to be the first in a series of gift books on American painters. The volume contains work by Rothermel, Thomas Sully, John Neagle, Samuel Waugh, Russell Smith, Thomas Buchanan Read, W. E. Winner, Joshua Shaw and S. S. Osgood.

Jean Froissart, a fourteenth-century French historian, who during the 1360s served as secretary to Queen Philippa of England, wife of Edward III, later wrote *The Chronicles of France, England, Scotland, and Spain*, which covers the years 1325–1400. Rothermel's painting shows Froissart reading his work (the word "Froissart" is visible on one page) to Philippa, described in the accompanying essay as "a favorable specimen of the noble dames of that age."[1] Since the *Chronicles* were written well after his service to the Queen, it is likely that Froissart is meant to be seen reading a preliminary history, his verse account of the Battle of Poitiers, or what were called "fine ditties and writings on love."[2]

This image of an elegant female monarch being read chivalric tales undoubtedly appealed to the gift book audience of the day. The caption to the engraving indicates that Rothermel's original painting was in the possession of J. B. Okie. The painting (unlocated) appeared in an exhibition at the Pennsylvania Academy of the Fine Arts in 1847, under the title *Froissart Reading His Chronicles to Queen Phillipa.*

[1] John S. Hart, "Froissart and His Chronicle," in John Sartain, ed., *The American Gallery of Art: From the Works of the Best Artists, with Poetical and Prose Illustrations, by Distinguished American Authors* (Philadelphia: Lindsay & Blakiston, 1848), p. 53.

[2] Jean Froissart, *Chronicles*, ed. Geoffrey Brereton (Hammondsworth, Eng.: Penguin Books, 1981), p. 12.

Maidenhood

Cat. 33
Maidenhood
John Sartain after
Peter F. Rothermel
1848
Engraving, 4³⁄₈ × 3³⁄₈ inches
(11.1 × 8.6 cm)
Published in *The Mirror of Life*
(Philadelphia: Lindsay &
Blakiston, 1848), p. 87.
Moore College of Art and
Design, Permanent Collection

The Mirror of Life and other popular gift books favored the type of sentimental image seen here. *Maidenhood* accompanied the story, "The Widower's Daughter" by Mrs. L. C. Tuthill. Two other illustrations by Rothermel appeared in the same volume: *Manhood* and *Old Age*.

The Pioneers [The Western Emigrants]

Cat. 34
The Pioneers [*The Western Emigrants*]
John Sartain after
Peter F. Rothermel
1849
Engraving,
4 × 6 inches (10.2 × 15.2 cm)
Published in *The Opal: A Pure Gift for All Seasons* (New York: J. C. Riker, 1849), facing p. 143.
Moore College of Art and Design, Permanent Collection

The settling of the West and frontier families were not subjects that Rothermel chose to paint; however, he did provide two such compositions for Sartain to engrave. The first—*Forest Worship*—appeared in *The Opal* in 1848 (fig. 23).[1] The image shows a frontier family, led by a Natty Bumppo–like father, about to cross a rude bridge. An accompanying poem refers to the man as a "knight" and to the forest glade as "sacred ground."[2] The family has built a sturdy log house and taken possession of the land. *The Pioneers*, which appeared in the same gift book the following year, shows a less heroic father and a family moving tentatively through the country. They still seek their destination. The composition anticipates, and perhaps influenced, George Caleb Bingham's painting *Daniel Boone Escorting the Settlers through the Cumberland Gap* (fig. 24).[3]

[1] This volume included seven other compositions drawn by Rothermel: *The Love of Tasso, Deborah's Triumph, The First Storm, Balboa, Naaman, The Elder Sister*, and the title page vignette. All were engraved by John Sartain.

[2] [Sarah J.] Hale, "Forest Worship," in *The Opal: A Pure Gift for the Holy Days* (New York: J. C. Riker, 1848), pp. 276–77.

[3] See E. Maurice Bloch, *George Caleb Bingham: The Evolution of an Artist* (Berkeley: University of California Press, 1967), p. 128, and J. Gray Sweeney, *The Columbus of the Woods: Daniel Boone and the Typology of Manifest Destiny* (St. Louis: Washington University Gallery of Art, 1992), p. 46. Bloch (p. 215) also makes connection between the two other works by the artists: Rothermel's drawing *The Angel of the Opal* (engraved frontis. by Sartain for *The Opal* of 1849) and Bingham's ca. 1862 painting *The Thread of Life*.

Fig. 23 *Forest Worship,*
John Sartain after Peter F. Rothermel
Engraving, 5 5/8 × 4 1/2 in. Moore College of Art and Design, Permanent Collection

Fig. 24 George Caleb Bingham, *Daniel Boone Escorting Settlers through the Cumberland Gap,* 1851-52, oil on canvas, 36 1/2 × 50 1/4 in. Washington University Gallery of Art, St. Louis, Missouri

Ruth and Boaz

Cat. 35
Ruth and Boaz
John Sartain after
Peter F. Rothermel
1849
Mezzotint engraving,
6 1/2 × 5 inches
(16.5 × 12.7 cm)
Published in *Sartain's Union
Magazine of Literature and Art* 4
(May 1849), frontis.
Moore College of Art and
Design, Permanent Collection

Fig. 25 *Ruth and Boaz*, 1849, John Sartain after
Peter F. Rothermel, stipple and mezzotint
engraving, 21 × 15 1/2 in. Robert Gordon Stewart

Rothermel painted two versions of *Ruth and Boaz*, and both were engraved by John Sartain. This engraving reproduces the now unlocated painting executed in 1845 and exhibited at the Pennsylvania Academy of the Fine Arts in 1847, at which time a Miss Stevens owned it.[1] When the print appeared in the May 1849 issue of *Sartain's Union Magazine of Literature and Art*, along with Lydia H. Signourney's poem "Ruth and Boaz," one S. Stevens was cited as possessing the original painting.

After viewing this "capital Picture" at Earles' gallery in Philadelphia in 1845, an impressed Joseph Sill decided to commission his own *Ruth and Boaz*.[2] Rothermel did not begin this work until 1847, finishing it the following year.[3] Sill's painting was exhibited at the Pennsylvania Academy in 1849 and Philadelphia's Great Central Fair of 1864.[4] The Philadelphia Art Union commissioned Sartain to engrave this version and distributed prints to its subscribers in 1849 (fig. 25).

The biblical story of Ruth and Boaz centers on loyalty and kindness. After Ruth's Israelite husband and father-in-law die in Moab, her homeland, Ruth accompanies her widowed mother-in-law, Naomi, to Israel. When the wealthy Boaz comes across Ruth gleaning in his field, Boaz inquires of his servant in charge of the reapers who she is. Upon learning her identity, Boaz praises her devotion to Naomi. She bows to the ground, "[a]nd when she was risen up to glean, Boaz commanded his young men saying, "Let her glean even among the sheaves, and do not reproach her" (Book of Ruth 2:15).[5]

Although both the Stevens and Sill compositions similarly represent the episode, the Stevens version depicts the figures at a slightly larger scale and more compactly grouped, with the kneeling overseer given a different orientation. Rothermel may have been inspired in his choice of subject, if not his composition, by Francis Wheatley's *Ruth and Boaz*, which had been reproduced in both a gift book, *The Rose of Sharon* (1842), and a journal, *Ladies' Companion* (1844).[6]

In addition to the two versions of *Ruth and Boaz*, Rothermel also painted *Ruth and Naomi*. The Pennsylvania Academy exhibited it, along with the Stevens painting, in 1847.

[1] The identity of Miss Stevens remains unknown; however, at midcentury the Misses Stevens and Aertson ran a school in Philadelphia; see Townsend Ward, "The Germantown Road and Its Associations," *Pennsylvania Magazine of History and Biography* 6 (1882): 276.

[2] September 8, 1845, Joseph Sill Diary, 6: 321, HSP.

[3] After examining a sketch for his composition, Sill mentioned in his diary that he had engaged Rothermel more than a year ago to execute the subject, "but which I did not press him to paint, as I have been rather more crampd than usual for funds." Sill was pleased with the finished product: "The Drawing is good, the colouring clear, well chosen, and rich with impasto; and the whole picture is a fit representation of the Scenery of an Oriental clime. It is a picture, I think of rare excellence; and the price quite moderately charged, because painted for me—say $125. The size is 36 inches by 29. It will enrich my Gallery" (September 1, 1847, and June 8, 1848, Sill Diary 7: 459, 8: 223).

[4] The Sill painting was auctioned by C. G. Sloan & Co. of Washington, D.C., in 1979.

[5] *Catalogue of the Twentieth-Sixth Annual Exhibition of the Pennsylvania Academy of the Fine Arts* (Philadelphia, 1849), p. 5.

[6] S. C. Edgarton, ed., *The Rose of Sharon* (Boston: A. Tompkins and B. B. Mussey, 1842): facing p. 76, engraved by E. Gallaudet. *Ladies' Companion* 20 (January 1844): frontis., engraved by Jordan and Halpin.

The Committee of Congress Drafting the Declaration of Independence

Cat. 36
The Committee of Congress Drafting the Declaration of Independence
T. D. Booth after
Peter F. Rothermel
Copyright 1865
Engraving,
29 3/4 × 23 7/8 inches
(75.6 × 60.6 cm)
The Library Company of
Philadelphia

This "beautiful engraving after a painting by Rothermel" was to be distributed to members of the Cincinnati-based Western Art-Union in 1852.[1] The same year, Rothermel's *De Soto Raising the Cross on the Banks of the Mississippi* (see cat. 7) was part of the art union's distribution of paintings. The subject of the print was timely, for Americans had recently celebrated the seventy-fifth anniversary of independence. The print seems not to have been distributed to the membership because of the art union's termination.[2] This would account for the print carrying a later copyright date.

The Committee of Congress Drafting the Declaration of Independence shows the same five men—Thomas Jefferson, John Adams, Benjamin Franklin, Robert Livingstone, and Roger Sherman—who are pictured in John Trumbull's famous and often reproduced image presenting their document to Congress. Unlike the formality and intellectual tenor of Trumbull's painting, Rothermel's composition offers a less focused episode. Indeed, a weakness of the composition is its lack of convincing interaction between the drafters. This additive character marks not only the figural arrangement, but also the uneasy relationship between heads and bodies. It seems apparent that Rothermel looked to portraits on which to base his likenesses, but he was not wholly successful in fitting bodies to those heads.

The work is somewhat unusual for Rothermel in that it does not render the emotional or confrontational moment so typical of his art. It concerns itself more with portraiture than a narrative and as such differs from his related painting *First Reading of the Declaration of Independence* (cat. 17).

[1] *North American and United States Gazette*, January 22, 1852, [p. 2]. The painting has no exhibition history and is unlocated today. Little is known of engraver T. Dwight Booth, who was working in Cincinnati in the early 1850s.

[2] Joy Sperling brought this information to my attention.

Landing of the Pilgrims

Cat. 37
Landing of the Pilgrims
Joseph Andrews after
Peter F. Rothermel
Copyright 1869
Steel engraving,
17 × 24¾ inches
(43.2 × 62.9 cm)
Thomas and Gail Bruhn

This impressive steel engraving by Joseph Andrews—considered his best work— appeared fifteen years after Rothermel had first exhibited the oil painting.[1] The circumstances surrounding the production of the engraving are not known, but the print became well known, attracted favorable notice from Earl Shinn and W. S. Baker, and was included in exhibitions at the Union League of Philadelphia (1873), the Metropolitan Museum of Art (1874), the Boston Art Club (1876), and the Centennial Exposition.[2]

Rothermel's sensational interpretation was less concerned with portraying the facts of history than in perpetuating its mythic dimensions. The grand histrionics of this romantic rendering proclaim the inspiration of Felicia Hemans's popular poem, "The Landing of the Pilgrim Fathers in New England" (1826):

> The breaking waves dash'd high
> On a stern and rock-bound coast,
> And the woods against a stormy sky
> Their giant branches toss'd:
> And the heavy night hung dark.
> The hills and water o'er,
> When a band of exiles moor'd their bark
> On the wild New England shore.[3]

Andrews's print appeared at a time when numerous chromolithographs pictured the dynamics of westward movement and settlement. These chromos, like the engraving, typically presented a historical perspective more ideal than real. The heroic determinism celebrated in *The Landing of the Pilgrims* takes its place then among the many contemporary images affirming America's Manifest Destiny.

---

[1] The painting is currently in the Kirby Collection, Lafayette College, Easton, Pa. Joseph Andrews worked in Boston. Matthias Baldwin, the first owner of the painting, apparently had commissioned it. On November 20, 1852, Joseph Sill (Diary, 10, 176, HSP) noted that Rothermel had "received an order to paint" the work.

[2] E. S., "Private Art-Collections of Philadelphia: X. Additional Galleries," *Lippincott's Magazine* 10 (December 1872): 710; W. S. Baker, *American Engravers and Their Works* (Philadelphia: Gebbie & Barrie, 1875), pp. 13–14; James L. Yarnall and William H. Gerdts, *The National Museum of American Art's Index to American Art Exhibition Catalogues: From the Beginning through the 1876 Centennial Year* (Boston: G. K. Hall, 1986), 1:109.

[3] *The Works of Felicia Hemans: Edited by Her Sister* (New York: C. S. Francis, 1849), p. 291.

Drawings

Cat. 38
Standing Male Holding a Staff
ca. 1849–1856
Inscribed (in another hand)
lower right:
    P.F.R.
Graphite and charcoal on paper,
mounted on cardboard,
25 × 14 inches
(63.5 × 35.6 cm)
Schwarz Gallery, Philadelphia

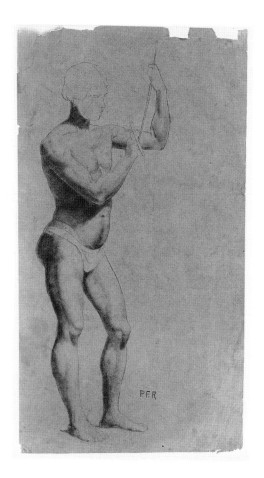

The practice of drawing from the live model lies at the core of the academic tradition. These life drawings of models striking stock poses, impressively reinforce Rothermel's commitment to and perpetuation of that tradition. The drawings, brought to varying degrees of finish, demonstrate the artist's understanding of human anatomy and his skill in articulating through line and shading what he saw.

The works were undoubtedly executed at the Graphic Club or the Pennsylvania Academy of the Fine Arts. At the first meeting of the Graphic Club on October 30, 1849, Rothermel was elected to chair the meeting. As chair, he stated the purpose of the club, which included promoting the arts by establishing schools for the study of the figure from life.[1] At the next meeting, November 12, Rothermel was elected president and named to the committee on the life class. The minutes for October 12, 1850, indicate the meeting was to take place at Rothermel's, but the members found the artist not there (twice) and were "suspicious that he was 'shirking.' " Nevetheless they talked of the life class having a male model one day, female another. A month later Samuel B. Waugh was elected president, with Rothermel remaining on the life class committee. Rothermel resigned from the club in 1851 (for reasons unknown). An intriguing entry in the club's minutes occurs on November 9, 1854: "At the request of Mr. Rothermel from the Academy of the Fine Arts a committee on Life Class was appointed." It is not clear whether this indicates that the Graphic Club's life class committee had disbanded when Rothermel quit or that Rothermel was attempting to involve the club more directly with the academy. It does show, however, his continuing commitment to the concept of the life class.

In 1854 Rothermel chaired the academy's Committee on Instruction, which presented to the Board the first clearly defined statement of what the Academy's curriculum should be. Modeled on the Ecole des Beaux-Arts, the curriculum included an award to be given to the best drawing from the antique and from the live model. Although Rothermel resigned as an academy director in 1855 (probably to prepare to go abroad), it was largely through his efforts that a new life class was established in the 1855–56 season and that the academy's first regularly scheduled life class occurred in the 1856–57 season.[2] Given his heightened interest in life studies during these years of involvement with the Graphic Club and the Pennsylvania Academy, it is most likely that these drawings date from the 1849–56.

Additionally, Elizabeth Milroy has noted that one of Rothermel's male models also appears in drawings by Christian Schuessele. Milroy suggests that the two artists hired the same model or even worked side by side.[3] That at least one drawing of the same female model was done by each artist further supports Milroy's suggestion. Schuessele and Rothermel were both involved in the Graphic Club. Schuessele, who joined the year Rothermel resigned, nominat-

Cat. 39
Female Nude Reclining
ca. 1849–1856
Inscribed (in another hand)
lower left:
    P.F.R.
Charcoal on paper
13 × 23¹/₂ inches
(33 × 59.7 cm)
Schwarz Gallery, Philadelphia

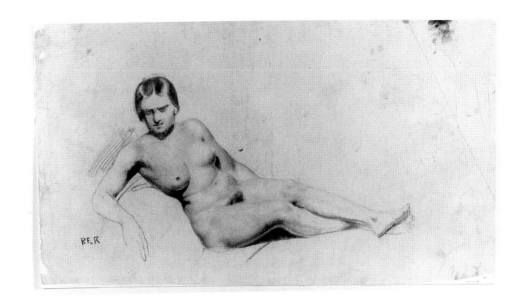

ed Rothermel for membership again in 1853.[4] Both artists appear on the club's records through 1855.

Former student of Thomas Eakins, Charles Bregler, found these six drawings among at least thirty life studies by Rothermel in the Eakins home in 1939 and carefully reported: "The life class drawings, up in the top studio are by Rothermel. I was careful these would not get out and passed off as Eakins."[5] Perhaps the "P.F.R." on each drawing, which seems not to be in the artist's hand, was Bregler's way of making certain they were not thought to be by Eakins. That the drawings were found among Eakins's effects is further evidence of the two men's artistic and personal relationship. The older artist likely served Eakins as a mentor, possibly as a teacher, and certainly as a friend. Eakins and Rothermel also were connected by their relationships with the Macdowell family (Rothermel's daughter married Eakins' wife's brother). These six drawings were given to photograher Carl Van Vechten by Susan Macdowell Eakins.[6]

[1] Minutes of the Proceedings of the Graphic Club, Graphic Association of Philadelphia 1849–1855, Sartain Family Collection, HSP. All of the following references to and quotations from the Graphic Club are taken from this source.

[2] Ronald J. Onorato, "The Pennsylvania Academy of the Fine Arts and the Development of an Academic Curriculum in the Nineteenth Century," Ph.D. diss., Brown University, 1977, pp. 54, 58–60.

[3] Elizabeth Lamotte Cates Milroy, "Thomas Eakins' Artistic Training, 1860–1870," Ph.D. diss., University of Pennsylvania, 1986, p. 61.

[4] November 17, 1853, Minutes of the Proceedings of the Graphic Club.

[5] Charles Bregler to Samuel Murray, July 23, 1939, as quoted in Kathleen Foster and Cheryl Liebold, *Writing About Eakins: The Manuscripts in Charles Bregler's Thomas Eakins Collection* (Philadelphia: University of Pennsylvania Press, 1989), p. 334.

[6] Milroy, "Thomas Eakins' Artistic Training," pp. 62, 61.

Cat. 40
Male Nude Facing Left
ca. 1849–1856
Inscribed (in another hand)
lower right:
  P.F.R.
Charcoal on paper,
24 × 18 inches (61 × 45.7 cm)
Schwarz Gallery, Philadelphia

Cat. 41
Seated Male Nude with Foot on Step
ca. 1849–1856
Inscribed (in another hand)
lower center, verso: P.F.R.
Charcoal on paper,
24 × 18¹/₂ inches
(61 × 47 cm)
Schwarz Gallery, Philadelphia

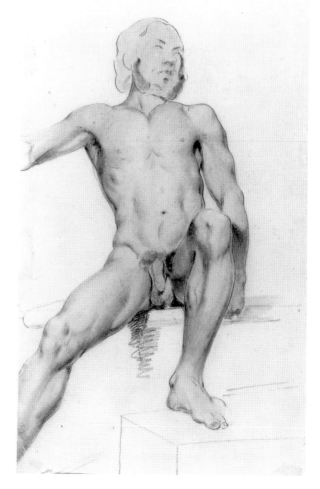

Cat. 42
Seated Male Nude Facing Right
ca. 1849–1856
Inscribed (in another hand)
lower right:
  P.F.R.
Charcoal and graphite on paper,
mounted on cardboard,
22 × 15 inches
(55.9 × 38.1 cm)
Schwarz Gallery, Philadelphia

Cat. 43
Seated Male Nude
ca. 1849–1856
Inscribed (in another hand)
lower right:
P.F.R.
Charcoal and graphite on paper,
mounted on cardboard,
20 × 13 1/2 inches
(50.8 × 34.3 cm)
Schwarz Gallery, Philadelphia

Study for King Lear and His Daughter

Cat. 44
Study for *King Lear and His Daughter*
1850
Inscribed lower right:
   P.F.R. Dem 23, 1850
Inscribed lower center:
   are these tears wet King Lear
Graphite on paper,
8 ⅞ × 11 ¾ inches
(22.5 × 29.8 cm)
Gil E. Pablo, M.D. Collection

This detailed drawing is a preliminary study for a painting exhibited at the Pennsylvania Academy of the Fine Arts in 1851 and again in 1862, at which time it was owned by James Lefevre. The picture than passed to W. P. Wilstach, who owned it at the time of Philadelphia's Great Central Fair in 1864. Today the painting—known as *King Lear and Cordelia*—is in a private collection.[1]

The subject derives from act 4, scene 7 of Shakespeare's *King Lear*. The tragic king, not in his "perfect mind," does nevertheless recognize his daughter Cordelia, who kneels before him and weeps on his hand. Behind the seated Lear stand two figures, presumably Kent and the doctor. In the painting, Rothermel focuses more attention on Cordelia and her father by increasing their scale and bringing them closer together, while eliminating the two standing figures and the tent setting. The tilt of Lear's head and his left hand are virtually identical in the painting and drawing. The compositional study offers a fine example of Rothermel's drawing ability and his skill in employing a variety of lines—from delicate to heavy—to define convincingly form and suggest space. The drawing differs significantly in subject and style from the *Lear and Cordelia* of a few years later (see cat. 61).

[1] Reproduced in Richard Studing, *Shakespeare in American Painting: A Catalogue from the Late Eighteenth Century to the Present* (Rutherford, N.J.: Fairleigh Dickinson University Press, 1993), no. 674.

Study for Rachel Bringing Laban to Jacob

Cat. 45
Study for *Rachel Bringing
Laban to Jacob*
1850
Inscribed lower left:
  PFR Dem 26, 1850
Inscribed lower right:
  Rachel bringing Laban to Jacob
Ink and wash on paper,
8 7/8 × 11 3/4 inches
(22.5 × 29.8 cm)
Gil E. Pablo, M.D. Collection

This drawing relates to an unlocated painting Joseph Sill mentioned in his diary. On March 14, 1849, Sill called on the artist "to see a picture he has nearly finished of the meeting of 'Jacob and Rachel,' painted for Mr. Potts; for which I was much pleased with, tho' I suggested some alterations." A month later, Sill again viewed the work, which he now called the *Meeting of Jacob and Rachel*, and deemed it "well illustrated—and altogether it is an agreeable production."[1] Once completed, the painting was apparently not exhibited, and it is unlocated today. Since no detailed description of its composition exists, the precise relationship of the painting to this drawing remains speculative; however, at least three possibilities exist. This highly finished sketch is a study (but dated later) for the painting; or it is a record Rothermel made of the completed painting; or it is a drawing for another picture.

The subject derives from Genesis. Jacob has rolled away a large stone from a well so that Rachel, whom he has just met, can water her sheep. After he tells Rachel that he is her father's kinsman, she runs off to inform her father. "When Laban heard the tidings of Jacob his sister's son, he ran to meet him, and embraced him and kissed him, and brought him to his house. Jacob told Laban all these things, and Laban said to him, 'Surely you are my bone and my flesh!' And he stayed with him a month" (Genesis 29:13–14). Later Jacob and Rachel marry. Rothermel's rendering shows not an ectastic meeting at the well, but one of restrained dignity.[2]

[1] March 14 and April 26, 1849, Joseph Sill Diary, 8: 448, 478, HSP.

[2] The restraint distinguishes the Rothermel drawing from an engraving after Schoppin's *Jacob & Rachel*, which served as the frontispiece to *Sartain's Union Magazine of Literature and Art* 5 (October 1849). In the engraving Jacob bows before Laban, who clasps his hand. Rothermel's Jacob is more aloof.

Flat Rock Bridge on the Schuylkill

Cat. 46
Flat Rock Bridge on the Schuylkill
1850
Inscribed lower left:
  Black Rock / Bridge / on the
  Schuylkill
Ink, wash, and graphite on paper,
8 7/8 × 11 3/4 inches
(22.5 × 29.8 cm)
Gil E. Pablo, M.D. Collection

Rothermel labeled this sketch "Black Rock Bridge," yet it depicts Flat Rock Bridge. No bridge at Black Rock is known to have existed; that at Flat Rock (near present-day Manayunk) opened in 1810 as the second permanent bridge in Philadelphia County. Another Rothermel drawing (in the Pennsylvania Academy of the Fine Arts) shows a similar composition and the same architectural forms, and that drawing is inscribed (in the artist's hand): "Flat Rock Bridge/Graphic Club." The Graphic Club, to which Rothermel belonged and served as its first president, made a sketching trip to Flat Rock on June 1, 1850. Rothermel participated in that sketching party.[1] Other members of the club at the time included Abraham Woodside, Paul Weber, Isaac Williams, Samuel Waugh, William Sanford Mason, Jacob Dallas, and James Hamilton.

[1] June 1, 1850, Minutes of the Proceedings of the Graphic Club, Graphic Association of Philadelphia, 1849–1855, Sartain Family Collection, HSP.

Study for Prejudice and Ill-Will Throwing Dirt on the Garments of Innocence

Cat. 47
Study for *Prejudice and Ill-Will Throwing Dirt on the Garments of Innocence*
1850
Inscribed lower right:
  PFR, Dem 29, 1850
Inscribed lower left:
  Prejudice an[d] Ill will casting
  dirt upon garments of
  Innocence / Pilgrims Progress
Inscribed upper left:
  ~~Wm Shuster~~/
  W. D. Kelly
Ink and wash on paper,
11 3/4 × 8 7/8 inches
(29.8 × 22.5 cm)
Gil E. Pablo, M.D. Collection

The unlocated painting to which this drawing relates appeared in the 1853 annual exhibition of the Pennsylvania Academy of the Fine Arts, at which time the Honorable William D. Kelly, Associate Justice of the Court of Common Pleas, Philadelphia, was listed as owner. Since this drawing is dated "1850" it is more likely a compositional study than a drawing reproducing the painting. It is also probable that the "W. D. Kelly" inscribed at the top, which Rothermel wrote in a larger hand, was added after the purchase of the painting as a record for the artist.

The subject derives from part 2 of John Bunyan's *Pilgrim's Progress* (1684), an enormously popular and influential book in nineteenth-century America. Images illustrating the book were common; for example, the Philadelphia Presbyterian Board of Publication issued thirteen folio size prints in 1844, and during the 1850s panoramas and gigantic paintings based on *Pilgrim's Progress* were popular entertainment.[1]

The passage that inspired Rothermel reads:

> Then they had them to another place, called *Mount-Innocent*. And there they saw a man cloathed all in White; and two men, *Prejudice*, and *Ill-will*, continually casting Dirt upon him. Now behold the Dirt, whatsoever they cast at him, would in little time fall off again, and his Garment would look as clear as if no Dirt had been cast thereat.

> Then said the Pilgrims what means this? The Shepherds answered, This man is named *Godly-man*, and this Garment is to shew the Innocency of his Life. Now those that throw Dirt at him, are such as hate his *Well-doing*, but as you see the Dirt will not stick upon his Clothes, so it shall be with him that liveth truly Innocently in the World. Whoever they be that would make such men dirty, they labor all in vain; for God, by that a little time is spent, will cause that their *Innocence* shall break forth as the Light, and their Righteousness as the Noon day.[2]

.Given the subject, that the painting went to a judge is entirely appropriate.

The head of Innocence resembles that of the divine form in Rothermel's *Hagar and the Angel* (cat. 6). The drawing is one of at least two *Pilgrim's Progress* scenes Rothermel sketched in a five-day period in 1850. Another drawing (collection of Gil E. Pablo, M.D.), dated December 24, represents the battle between Christian and the monster Apollyon.

---

[1] David E. Smith, "Illustrations to American Editions of *The Pilgrim's Progress* to 1870," *Princeton University Chronicle* 26 (Autumn 1964): 21.

[2] John Bunyan, *The Pilgrim's Progress from the World to That Which Is to Come*, ed. James Blanton Wharey and Roger Sharrock (2d ed., rev.; Oxford: Oxford University Press, 1960), pp. 285–86.

(Cat. 47)

Head of a Woman

Cat. 48
Head of a Woman
1850
Inscribed lower center:
  PFR 1850
Ink, wash, and graphite on paper,
11¾ × 8⅞ inches
(29.8 × 22.5 cm)
Gil E. Pablo, M.D. Collection

"Lucifer as the Angel of Revolt"

Cat. 49
"Lucifer as the Angel of Revolt"
ca. 1850
Inscribed lower center:
  Lucifer as / the Angel of Revolt /
  Communion of the *Poor*
Ink, wash, and graphite on paper,
11¾ × 8⅞ inches
(29.8 × 22.5 cm)
Gil E. Pablo, M.D. Collection

This drawing is intriguing not only in showing Rothermel's facility in handling a variety of media for differing effects, but also in presenting a unique subject. While the Bible, John Milton, and John Bunyan would seem to be likely sources of the subject, none apparently is, and Rothermel's inspiration remains unknown. The drawing may relate to the artist's allegorical painting, *The Laborer's Vision of Human Progress* (1851, unlocated). Lucifer, who kneels in the picture, has variously described as the "ANGEL OF FREEDOM" and the "Spirit of Evil repentant."[1] The turrets of a medieval castle are also apparent. Although descriptions of *The Laborer's Vision of Human Progress* chronicle a composition markedly different from that of the drawing, its treatment of the poor and inclusion of Lucifer suggest a kinship with the sketch.

[1] "Rothermel's Last Picture," *Philadelphia Art Union Reporter* 1 (January 1851): 19; James L. Yarnall and William H. Gerdts, *The National Museum of American Art's Index to American Art Exhibition Catalogues: From the Beginning through the 1876 Centennial Year* (Boston: G. K. Hall, 1986), 4:3061. The latter phrase appeared in an 1853 exhibition catalogue for the Massachusetts Academy of Fine Arts [Boston].

"Angels Who Rejoice over Repentance"

Cat. 50
"Angels Who Rejoice over Repentance"
ca. 1850
Inscribed lower right:
  For the angels who rejoice over
  Repentance cannot be heal
  pain / as they try and try again
  in vain, whether they may not
  harm / kind hearts with the
  brooding of their kind
  beings. / Mr. Ruskin
Ink and wash on paper,
$8\,7/8 \times 11\,3/4$ inches
$(22.5 \times 29.8$ cm)
Gil E. Pablo, M.D. Collection

"The Artist's Studio"

Cat. 51
"The Artist's Studio"
ca. 1850–1853
Inscribed lower right:
  Artist Studio/
  P.F. Rothermel artist
Ink and wash on paper,
$8\,7/8 \times 11\,3/4$ inches
$(22.5 \times 29.8$ cm)
Gil E. Pablo, M.D. Collection
See. fig. 8.

Study for John Balfour of Burley in the Cave

Cat. 52
Study for *John Balfour of Burley in the Cave*
ca. 1852
Inscribed lower left:
   Balfour of Burl / Old Mortality
Ink, wash, and graphite on paper,
8 7/8 × 11 3/4 inches
(22.5 × 29.8 cm)
Gil E. Pablo, M.D. Collection

John Balfour of Burley is a character from Sir Walter Scott's Waverley novel, *Old Mortality*, an 1816 book that had earlier inspired Rothermel's *Death of Old Mortality* (shown in the Artists' Fund Society exhibition of 1841). The tale chronicles the religious persecution of the seventeenth-century Convenanters (Presbyterians) who refused to acknowledge royal authority. Burley, an extremist Convenanter, had murdered the head of the Scottish Episcopal Church, Archbishop Sharpe of Saint Andrews. Near the novel's conclusion, the deranged Burley hides:

Burley, only altered from what he had been formerly by the addition of a grisly beard, stood in the midst of the cave, with his clasped Bible in one hand, and his drawn sword in the other. His figure, dimly ruddied by the light of the red charcoal, seemed that of a fiend in the lurid atmosphere of Pandemonium, and his gestures and words, as far as they could be heard, seemed equally violent and irregular. All alone, and in a place of almost unapproachable seclusion, his demeanor was that of a man who strives for life and death with a mortal enemy. "Ha! ha!—there—there!," he exclaimed, accompnaying each word with a thrust, urged with his whole force against the impassable and empty air—"Did I not tell thee so?—I have resisted, and thou fleest from!—Coward as thou art—come in all thy terrors—come with mine own evil deeds, which render thee most terrible of all—there is enough betwixt the boards of this book to rescue me!—What mutterest thou of grey hairs!—It was well done to slay him—the more ripe the corn, the readier for the sickle.—Art gone? art gone?—I have ever known thee but a coward—ha! ha! ha!"[1]

Scott's crazed Burley offered an ideal subject for Rothermel, who had a penchant for dynamic renderings of agitated figures. In this drawing, a few quick touches created the illusion of the cave, while contrasting heavy and subtle strokes and washes conveyed Burley's psychological turmoil.

The sketch undoubtedly served as a study for the artist's *John Balfour of Burley in the Cave* (unlocated). The Art Union of Philadelphia included this painting as part of its distribution of 1853; it went to Daniel J. Morrell of Philadelphia.

[1] Walter Scott, *Waverley Novels* (New York: Collins, n.d.), 2:731.

"Factory Life"

Cat. 53
"Factory Life"
1852
Inscribed lower center:
  Factory *Life*/1852
Ink and wash on paper,
8 ⁷⁄₈ × 11 ³⁄₄ inches
(22.5 × 29.8 cm)
Gil E. Pablo, M.D. Collection

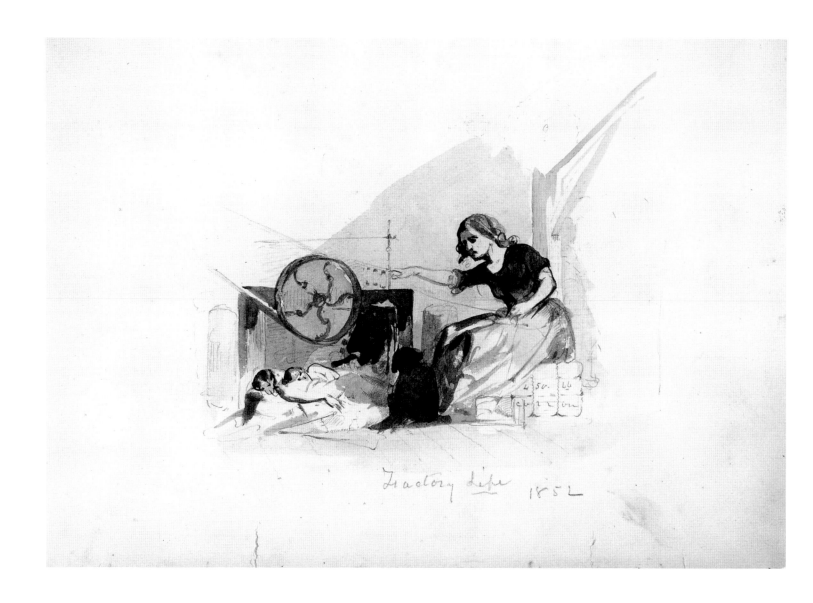

Study for Antonio's Letter

Cat. 54
Study for *Antonio's Letter*
1853
Inscribed lower center:
  Bassano & Portia
Inscribed lower right:
  Painted for, Joseph Sill
  Esq / 1853
Ink, wash, and graphite on paper,
8 7/8 × 11 3/4 inches
(22.5 × 29.8 cm)
Gil E. Pablo, M.D. Collection

The unlocated painting for which this is a study appeared in the 1853 Pennsylvania Academy of the Fine Arts annual exhibition. Its catalogue entry included a passage from Shakespeare's *Merchant of Venice*:

> *Portia.* There are shome shrewd contents in yon same paper,
> That steal the color from Bassanio's cheek.
> ★ ★ ★
> What! worse and worse! with leave Bassanio—[1]

In his diary, Joseph Sill, who commissioned the painting, left a particularly informative account of the circumstances of its creation:

April 5, 1851: Sill arranges with Rothermel to paint a picture of a scene from the "Merchant of Venice" selected by Sill. The work is to be executed within the year. Rothermel has received many commissions and Sill notes: "I am truly glad that so good an Artist is becoming so much appreciated."

May 3, 1851: Mr. and Mrs. Sill and their son attend a performance of the "Merchant of Venice" at the Walnut Street Theatre.[2]

October 19, 1852: "In the afternoon I went to see Mr. Rothermel the Artist and took with me Knight's Pictorial Shakespeare containing the 'Merchant of Venice' that he might study the part which I wish him to illustrate for me—there are hints for Costume in it which may be valueable to him. He is complaining of the weakness in his eyes."[3]

February 9, 1853: Sill calls on the artist and is "glad to find that he has commenced my Picture of "Bassanio reading Antonio's Letter", and that its composition & colour gave me great pleasure: for altho' the Picture is yet in the first painting it gives forcible evidence that he has illustrated the story with remarkable clearness, and has chosen an arrangement of background, costume etc. which add great effect to the story. So far it surpasses my expectation: and *that* was considerably great."

February 25, 1853: Sill sees that the picture "was advancing in a very pleasing manner—he [Rothermel] wishes to send it to the Exhibition in April next."

March 8, 1853: Sill orders a frame.

March 11, 1853: Sill calls on Rothermel to check frame. He is not satisfied because the frame has too much "curve in the upper part next to the Picture."

March 19, 1853: Sill calls on the artist to see the picture finished, but it is not.

March 26, 1853: With his wife, Sill visits Rothermel to look at the picture. Mrs. Sill likes it, but suggests "certain modifications etc."

April 6, 1853: Sill calls on Rothermel and finds that he has changed the color of Bassanio's costume, which he considers "a deterioration"

Bassano & Portia

Painted for Joseph Gillott
1858.

Rothermel changes it to another color more in harmony with the rest. Rothermel has not progressed as much as Sill anticipated; he has been busy with portraiture.

April 13, 1853: Sill visits the studio. He is pleased with the painting and thinks it will make a handsome pendent to his *Ruth and Boaz* (fig. 25). He tells Rothermel two or three points which need to be amended, which Rothermel agrees to do.

April 20, 1853: With Rothermel, Sill goes to the Pennsylvania Academy of the Fine Arts. The artist wants to retouch the painting because it will lack "strength" when exhibited. He wishes Sill to see it again before the exhibition.

April 26, 1853: Sill calls on Rothermel to see the last touches on the picture "which I thought now as good as it can be."

April 30, 1853: Sill meets with Rothermel at the academy to look at the painting, which Rothermel says he will retouch some more. While there they meet Mr. Gratz and Sill asks him his opinion of the work. "but it never occurred to me until I left the Academy that Mr. Gratz, as a Jew, might feel some objection to the subject, which shows the effect of the Jew Shylock's purposed revenge on the Merchant of Venice; and feeling thus I immediately wrote to Mr. Rothermel to keep it out of the Exhibition altogether if he thought it might produce *any* unpleasant sensation."[4]

May 3, 1853: Sill visits Rothermel and sees that the painting is much improved. Rothermel does not think that Gratz had any objection and plans to send it to the exhibition.

May 9, 1853: The painting is included in the Academy exhibition, but not hung in a good light. Rothermel will make some alterations in the painting. "Mrs. S. is not satisfied with some of the parts, but I think she is a severe critic."

August 9, 1853: Rothermel retouches the picture because he wants to "do it justice."

June 24, 1854: Rothermel calls on Sill to look at "Portia and Bassanio" for the purpose of slightly retouching it.

---

[1] *Catalogue of the Thirtieth Annual Exhibition of the Pennsylvania Academy of the Fine Arts* (Philadelphia, 1853), p. 5 no. 68. The passage is from act 3, scene 2. Rothermel executed at least two other paintings taken from the "Merchant of Venice": *Judgment Scene from the Merchant of Venice* (1849, unlocated), *Shylock and Jessica* (1866?, unlocated).

[2] This entry and the one above are from pp. 329 and 346 of volume 9 of the Joseph Sill Diary, HSP. The following entries occur in volume 10 on pp. 154, 227, 239, 245, 246, 252, 256, 263, 267, 272, 279, 281, 282, 518.

[3] Sill is referring to Charles Knight, ed., *The Pictorial Edition of the Works of William Shakespeare* (London: C. Knight, 1839–43). Why there is no mention of the painting for almost 1 1/2 years is unknown, although his comment about Rothermel's complaint about his eyes may be a clue. Perhaps the artist suffered some debilitating illness; indeed, no paintings by the artist are known to date from 1852.

[4] Most likely this was Hyman Gratz, who served as a director of the Pennsylvania Academy of the Fine Arts (1836–57) and its treasurer (1841–57). At the time the Gratzes "constituted what was doubtless the foremost Jewish family…in the United States" (David Philipson, *Letters of Rebecca Gratz* (Philadelphia: Jewish Publication Society of America, 1929), p. xi) and Hyman Gratz was "the family's chief representative in art circles" (Edwin Wolf 2nd and Maxwell Whiteman, *The History of the Jews of Philadelphia from Colonial Times to the Age of Jackson* [Philadelphia: Jewish Publication Society of America, 1975], p. 323).

"David Playing before Saul"

Cat. 55
"David Playing before Saul"
ca. 1852
Inscribed lower center:
  David Playing / before Saul /
  Saul & David
Ink, wash, and graphite on paper,
8 ⅞ × 11 ¾ inches
(22.5 × 29.8 cm)
Gil E. Pablo, M.D. Collection

"David and Saul"

Cat. 56
"David and Saul"
ca. 1852–1853
Graphite on paper,
8 ⅞ × 11 ¾ inches
(22.5 × 29.8 cm)
Gil E. Pablo, M.D. Collection

This drawing was, presumably, executed in preparation for an oil painting; however, the literature on Rothermel and surviving exhibition records do not mention a *David and Saul.* The drawing, showing a fine range of touch and finish, probably was rendered about the same time as *David Playing the Harp before Saul* (cat. 10) and may have been intended as a companion picture. The subject is taken from I Samuel 26:7–12:

> So David and Abishai went to the army by night; and there lay Saul sleeping within the encampment, with his spear stuck in the ground at his head; and Abner and the army lay around him. Then said Abishai to David, "God has given your enemy into your hand this day; now therefore let me pin him to the earth with one stroke of the spear, and I will not strike him twice." But David said to Abishai, "Do not destroy him; for who can put forth his hand against the LORD's anointed, and be guiltless?"...The LORD forbid that I should put forth my hand against the LORD's anointed; but take now the spear that is at his head, and the jar of water, and let us go." So David took the spear and the jar of water from Saul's head; and they went away. No man saw it, or knew it, nor did any awake; for they were all asleep, because of a deep sleep from the LORD had fallen upon them.

"The Grandfather"

Cat. 57
"The Grandfather"
ca. 1850–1853
Inscribed lower center:
    The Grandfather
Ink, wash, and graphite on paper,
8 7/8 × 11 3/4 inches
(22.5 × 29.8 cm)
Gil E. Pablo, M.D. Collection

Study for Thou Art the Man

Cat. 58
Study for *Thou Art the Man*
ca. 1853
Inscribed lower left to center:
    & Nathan Said unto David /
    Thou Art the Man
Graphite on paper,
8 7/8 × 11 3/4 inches
(22.5 × 29.8 cm)
Gil E. Pablo, M.D. Collection

Study for Thou Art the Man

Cat. 59
Study for *Thou Art the Man*
ca. 1853
Inscribed lower center:
  Thou Art the Man
Graphite on paper,
8 7/8 × 11 3/4 inches
(22.5 × 29.8 cm)
Gil E. Pablo, M.D. Collection

Woman Facing Left

Cat. 60
Woman Facing Left
ca. 1850–1855
Ink and wash on paper,
11 3/4 × 8 7/8 inches
(29.8 × 22.5 cm)
Gil E. Pablo, M.D. Collection

Lear and Cordelia

Cat. 61
Lear and Cordelia
1855
Inscribed lower right:
  P. F. Rothermel 1855
Ink and ink wash on blue-gray
wove paper,
14 ³/₄ × 20 ⁹/₁₆ inches
(37.5 × 52.2 cm)
Museum of American Art of
the Pennsylvania Academy
of the Fine Arts, Philadelphia;
gift of Saul and Ellin Lapp

This impressively rendered drawing relates to Rothermel's *The Last Scene in Lear*, which was shown in the 1856 annual exhibition of the National Academy of Design. The painting, owned by Edward P. Mitchell, also appeared in exhibitions at the Pennsylvania Academy of the Fine Arts (1857 and 1861) and the Pittsburgh Art Association (1860). The Pittsburgh catalogue included the text of act 5 scene 3 from Shakespeare's *King Lear* in the entry for the painting.[1]

The drawing expressively conveys the king's anguish over the death of his daughter, Cordelia:

> *Lear.*Howl, howl, howl, howl! O, you are men of stones:
> Had I your tongues and eyes, I'd use them
> That heaven's vault should crack. She's gone for ever![2]

The drawing may be more successful than the now unlocated painting. A reviewer of the National Academy exhibition decided the painting treated the subject in a "terrible manner" and likened the figures's bulging eyes to those of lobsters, even though, so the writer conceeded, Rothermel possessed "great facility of drawing."[3]

[1] James L. Yarnall and William H. Gerdts, *The National Museum of American Art's Index to American Art Exhibition Catalogues: From the Beginning through the 1876 Centennial Year* (Boston: G. K. Hall, 1986), 4:3058. The exhibition at the Great Central Fair (1864) included 2 Rothermel paintings titled *Lear and Cordelia*—one owned by W. P. Wilstach (cat. 44), and the other by Col. Cephas Childs. Since Rothermel is only known to have painted two scenes of Lear and Cordelia, I presume Childs's picture was the one Mitchell had previously owned.

[2] William George Clark and William Aldis Wright, *The Complete Works of William Shakespeare* (New York: Grosset & Dunlap, 1911), pp. 1091–92.

[3] "The National Academy of Design," *New-York Daily Tribune*, April 12, 1856, p. 4.

Study of a Head of a Woman

Cat. 62
Study of a Head of a Woman
ca. 1857
Oil on paper, 9 × 7 3/4 inches
(22.9 × 19.7 cm)
Gil E. Pablo, M.D. Collection

This impressive study relates to an ink and graphite drawing in the collections of the Munson-Williams-Proctor Institute that shows a woman holding a bundle of sticks (fig. 26).[1] The correspondence between the heads of the women in the drawing and oil study is striking. Since the drawing bears an inscription indicating that it was executed in Genazzano in July 1857, the oil study is presumed also to have been created in this Italian village where Rothermel had a studio.

The study is one of several stylistically similar oil sketches, which include another image of the same woman (see cat. 63). Likely all were made in Italy, and all are noteworthy for their convincing sense of form and individual character.

[1] Paul D. Schweitzer kindly brought this drawing to my attention and shared his research with me.

Fig. 26 Peter F. Rothermel, *Italian Woman Holding a Bundle of Wood,* 1857, ink and graphite on gray paper, 11 × 8 1/4 in. Munson-Williams-Proctor Institute Museum of Art; Museum purchase

Study of a Head of a Woman

Cat. 63
Study of a Head of a Woman
ca. 1857
Oil on paper,
7 ³/₄ × 5 ¹/₂ inches
(19.7 × 14 cm)
Gil E. Pablo, M.D. Collection

Study of a Head of a Woman Turned to the Right

Cat. 64
Study of a Head of a Woman Turned to the Right
ca. 1857
Oil on canvas,
7 ¹/₈ × 5 ¹/₈ inches
(18.1 × 13 cm)
Gil E. Pablo, M.D. Collection

Study of Head of a Bearded Man

Cat. 65
Study of Head of a Bearded Man
ca. 1857
Oil on paper,
8 ¹/₈ × 7 ¹/₄ inches
(20.6 × 18.4 cm)
Gil E. Pablo, M.D. Collection

Study of a Head of a Mustachioed Man in a Hat

Cat. 66
*Study of a Head of a Mustachioed
Man in a Hat*
ca. 1857
Oil on paper,
9 ¹/₂ × 7 ³/₄ inches
(24.1 × 19.7 cm)
Gil E. Pablo, M.D. Collection

Study of a Head of a Man in Historical Costume

Cat. 67
*Study of a Head of a Man in
Historical Costume*
ca. 1857
Oil on paper, 9 × 7 ⅞ inches
(22.9 × 20 cm)
Gil E. Pablo, M.D. Collection

Study of a Head of a Man Turned to the Right

Cat. 68
*Study of a Head of a Man Turned
to the Right*
ca. 1857
Oil on canvas,
8 3/4 × 7 1/2 inches
(22.2 × 19 cm)
Gil E. Pablo, M.D. Collection

Study of a Head of a Young Man Turned to the Left

Cat. 69
*Study of a Head of a Young Man
Turned to the Left*
ca. 1857
Oil on paper, 8 × 5 1/2 inches
(20.3 × 14 cm)
Gil E. Pablo, M.D. Collection

Two Studies of a Young Man's Head

Cat. 70
Two Studies of a Young Man's Head
ca. 1857
Oil on canvas, 7 ¼ × 9 inches
(18.4 × 22.9 cm)
Gil E. Pablo, M.D. Collection

Three Studies of Hands

Cat. 71
Three Studies of Hands
ca. 1857
Oil on canvas,
5 ½ × 8 ¼ inches
(14 × 20.9 cm)
Gil E. Pablo, M.D. Collection

Study for Christ and the Three Marys

Cat. 72
Study for *Christ and the
Three Marys*
ca. 1858
Ink, wash, and graphite on paper,
8 ⁷⁄₈ × 11 ³⁄₄ inches
(22.5 × 29.8 cm)
Gil E. Pablo, M.D. Collection

The Rothermel painting *The Three Marys at the Sepulchre*, then owned by J. J. Gilliams, was included in the 1858 Pennsylvania Academy of the Fine Arts annual exhibition. The following year the painting was included in the third annual exhibition of the Washington Art Association. Presumably, this drawing relates to that unlocated painting.

Gilliams's name appears in Rothermel's notebook with other patrons who had commissioned work before the artist sailed to Europe in 1856. A purchase price of $250 was set, with the subject left to Rothermel. Also in the notebook, under the heading "1858," is a list of numerous biblical episodes (probably as potential painting subjects), including Christ and the three Marys.[1]

[1] "1858," Rothermel notebook.

"Rubens Presenting His 'Descent from the Cross'"

Cat. 73

"Rubens Presenting His 'Descent from the Cross'"
ca. 1858
Watercolor and graphite on buff
wove paper,
9 7/8 × 12 1/8 inches
(25.1 × 30.8 cm)
Museum of American Art of
the Pennsylvania Academy
of the Fine Arts, Philadelphia;
gift of Saul and Ellin Lapp

This highly realized composition study relates to Rothermel's *Rubens and Van Dyck* (1858, unlocated) which Russian Prince Kozebue had commissioned in Rome. Another version of the painting was included in the 1858 annual exhibition of the Pennsylvania Academy of the Fine Arts. Among materials owned by Rothermel now in the Pennsylvania Academy is an engraving after Rubens's *Descent from the Cross.*

Study of a Soldier for Battle of Gettysburg: Pickett's Charge

Cat. 74
Study of a Soldier for *Battle of Gettysburg: Pickett's Charge*
1867–1870
Graphite on paper,
7 3/4 × 9 1/4 inches
(19.7 × 23.5 cm)
Gil E. Pablo, M.D. Collection